Cambridge Elements

Elements in World Englishes
edited by
Edgar W. Schneider
University of Regensburg

MULTISCRIPTAL ENGLISH IN TRANSLITERATED LINGUISTIC LANDSCAPES

Chonglong Gu
The Hong Kong Polytechnic University

Shaftesbury Road, Cambridge CB2 8EA, United Kingdom

One Liberty Plaza, 20th Floor, New York, NY 10006, USA

477 Williamstown Road, Port Melbourne, VIC 3207, Australia

314–321, 3rd Floor, Plot 3, Splendor Forum, Jasola District Centre, New Delhi – 110025, India

103 Penang Road, #05–06/07, Visioncrest Commercial, Singapore 238467

Cambridge University Press is part of Cambridge University Press & Assessment, a department of the University of Cambridge.

We share the University's mission to contribute to society through the pursuit of education, learning and research at the highest international levels of excellence.

www.cambridge.org
Information on this title: www.cambridge.org/9781009490023
DOI: 10.1017/9781009490054

© Chonglong Gu 2025

This publication is in copyright. Subject to statutory exception and to the provisions of relevant collective licensing agreements, no reproduction of any part may take place without the written permission of Cambridge University Press & Assessment.

When citing this work, please include a reference to the DOI 10.1017/9781009490054

First published 2025

A catalogue record for this publication is available from the British Library

ISBN 978-1-009-49006-1 Hardback
ISBN 978-1-009-49002-3 Paperback
ISSN 2633-3309 (online)
ISSN 2633-3295 (print)

Cambridge University Press & Assessment has no responsibility for the persistence or accuracy of URLs for external or third-party internet websites referred to in this publication and does not guarantee that any content on such websites is, or will remain, accurate or appropriate.

Multiscriptal English in Transliterated Linguistic Landscapes

Elements in World Englishes

DOI: 10.1017/9781009490054
First published online: January 2025

Chonglong Gu
The Hong Kong Polytechnic University

Author for correspondence: Chonglong Gu, Chonglong.Gu@polyu.edu.hk

Abstract: In this Element, 'multiscriptal English' is theorised. Unorthodox and unconventional this may sound, a salient sociolinguistic reality is emerging globally. That is, while standardised English (Roman script) is routinely taught and used, English in superdiverse, multilingual and/or (post)colonial societies is often camouflaged in local scripts and 'passes off' as local languages in these places' linguistic landscapes through transliteration (at lexical, phrasal and sentential levels). To illustrate, documentary evidence from Arabic, Malay (Jawi), Nepali, Urdu, Tamil, Korean, Japanese, Russian, Thai and so on is presented. Through inter-scriptal rendition, English is glocalised and enshrined in seemingly 'exotic' scripts that embody different sociopolitical and religious worldviews. In the (re)contextualisation process, English inevitably undergoes transformations and adopts new flavours. This gives English a second life with multiple manifestations/incarnations in new contexts. This points to the juggernaut of English in our globalised/neoliberal world. The existence of multiscriptal English necessitates more coordinated and interdisciplinary research efforts going forward.

Keywords: world Englishes, multiscriptal English, globalisation, neoliberalism, transliteration, translation, inter-scriptal rendition

© Chonglong Gu 2025

ISBNs: 9781009490061 (HB), 9781009490023 (PB), 9781009490054 (OC)
ISSNs: 2633-3309 (online), 2633-3295 (print)

Contents

1. Introduction: Setting the Scene — 1
2. Major Perspectives to Studying English: From Overt and Explicit Use to Covert and Implicit Use — 3
3. Multiscriptal English Theorised: English Glocalised and Transliterated in Other Languages/Scripts — 5
4. Multiscriptal English, Translanguaging, Multilingualism and Lexical Borrowing — 7
5. Linguistic Landscape (LL) as Theoretical Framework, Methodology and Vivid Site to Studying Evolving English in Action — 9
6. The Translational and Cross-Linguistic Aspect of the Making of (Multilingual) Linguistic Landscapes — 13
7. Multiscriptal English in Action: Evidence from Multiple Languages and Scripts around the World — 14
8. Transliterated Globalisation: Some Reflections — 99
9. Discussions and Concluding Remarks — 102

References — 108

1 Introduction: Setting the Scene

This Element advances scholarship by highlighting and revealing an important multilingual and multiscriptal dimension to English, that is, the all-powerful English is increasingly written in different scripts and often passes off as a 'local' language in our globalised world. Despite its somewhat (inglorious) past as the colonial language of the British Empire and the language of military expansion (Crystal 1997; Crystal 2004), this West Germanic language English has, for various historical, political and socio-economic reasons (Bolton 2012; Crystal 1997; 2004; Kachru 1992; Kirkpatrick 2021), risen to global prominence as the single most dominant and powerful language (Bolton and Jenks 2022; Deterding 2005; Kirkpatrick 2007; Pandey 2020; Schneider 2007; Siemund, Al-Issa and Leimgruber 2021) across the globe at an unprecedented level. Now, in our globalised, neoliberal and interconnected world featuring increasing superdiversity (Blommaert 2013; Piller 2018; Vertovec 2007), English effectively serves as the bridge, permitting effective communication and meaningful contact to take place between people from diverse ethnic, linguistic and cultural backgrounds in such domains as diplomacy, politics, media, journalism, business, commerce, culture, education and technology. If our multilingual world may be seen as a 'linguistic market' (Bourdieu 1977), English is definitely the most important language and the one and only global *lingua franca* in the true sense of the word. Around the world, the English language is increasingly perceived as an index of globalisation, development, modernity, progress, cosmopolitanism, open-mindedness, liberalism, sophistication and even good taste (Gu and Almanna 2023; Lanza and Woldemariam 2014; Manan and Hajar 2022; Piller 2003).

Given its growing importance, English has now attracted increasing scholarly attention from a range of angles and perspectives, which have pointed towards the juggernaut of English and its powerful and instrumental nature in our world for various sociopolitical, economic, institutional, communicative, commercial, educational and symbolic functions. Particularly notably, over the years, world Englishes (WE) has consolidated itself as a dominant area dedicated to exploring the historical developments as well as the current role, relevance and significance of English in a highly contextualised, glocalised and nuanced way (Bolton and Jenks 2022; Boyle 2011; Crystal 1997; Filppula, Klemola, and Sharma 2017; Kachru 1992; Kachru, Kachru, and Nelson 2006; Kirkpatrick 2021; Kortmann and Schneider 2004; Meierkord and Schneider 2021; Mesthrie 2019; Pandey 2020; Schneider 2007; Schreier, Hundt, and Schneider 2020; Sharifian 2010). Essentially interdisciplinary in nature, world Englishes (WE), as a line of research, is particularly interested in and attentive to exploring how

English has over time become indigenised and taken on local/regional flavours in a wide range of sociopolitical, geographical, ethnolinguistic and cultural contexts through language contact at various levels.

To date, WE researchers have, amongst others, described and documented local varieties of English in post-colonial or outer-circle societies such as Hong Kong, Singapore, Malaysia, Fiji, the Philippines, Nigeria, Jamaica, India, Sri Lanka and Pakistan. Increasingly, different varieties of English are explored in expanding-circle societies such as Japan, China, Thailand, South Korea, Cambodia, Russia, Kazakhstan, Italy, France, Hungary, Belgium, Greece, Poland and Brazil (e.g. Djuraeva 2021; Grigg 1997; Griffin 1997; Hilgendorf 2007; Pétery 2011; Seargeant 2005; Snodin 2014), which are places without traditional colonial ties with the British Empire.

Despite such efforts in exploring different aspects of English in various geographical and sociocultural contexts, almost all studies so far have focused on spoken varieties of English and also English(es) written in the Roman script – which represent the traditional, conventional, standard, purist and idealised understanding of the English language (Hackert 2012; Wright 2000). As such, there is a significant lack of attention to the multiscriptal aspect of the English language. Against a backdrop of globalisation, language contact and neoliberalism, there is an increasingly visible trend globally that English is (re)contextualised in local languages and transliterated into local scripts in an inter-scriptal manner at lexical, phrasal and sentential levels. That is, through phonetic transliteration, the all-powerful English can have multiple manifestations or 'faces', becoming camouflaged in and passing off as other less dominant and even seemingly 'exotic' languages in our (post)colonial and/or globalised societies.

Employing seemingly inscrutable, 'exotic' and 'mysterious' non-Roman writing systems (e.g. the Arabic, Devanagari, Korean and Cyrillic scripts), these languages are linguistically and historically far removed from English, which embody and project dissimilar, if not diametrically different, sociopolitical worldviews, cultural values and religious beliefs. Through inter-scriptal transliteration, English makes inroads into other languages in an implicit and covert way at an unprecedented level. The pervasive use of transliteration blurs the traditional boundaries between formally named languages, thus giving rise to new varieties and new identities. The main focus of this work is to illustrate the multilingual and multiscriptal dimensions of English, beyond English in the conventional sense.

Drawing on real-world multilingual data amassed from various geographical, linguistic and sociopolitical contexts, this Element contributes to World Englishes (WE) scholarship and beyond from an innovative multiscriptal and cross-lingual perspective. Linguistic landscape (cf. Ben-Rafael et al. 2006; Coluzzi 2016; Landry and Bourhis 1997; Spolsky and Cooper 1991) is employed here both as a source of theoretical insights, methodology and a vivid site to study the constantly evolving English in action in a changing context. Our linguistic landscape represents a dynamic space where various languages are showcased and displayed and compete for attention. Documentary data from such languages as Arabic, Malay, Tamil, Nepali, Urdu, Thai, Korean, Japanese and Russian are presented and discussed as case studies. I will highlight how changes might be introduced in the inter-scriptal transliteration process. That is, due to the inherent linguistic and scriptal differences and individuals' different and subjective understandings of English and various scripts involved, English may take on new flavours and have new identities in the new environments after the (re)contextualisation process. Also, two important notions 'multiscriptal English' and 'transliterated globalisation' are theorised to help capture this relatively novel and fascinating phenomenon potentially with far-reaching ramifications. Going from the overt and explicit to the hidden and covert use of English, this Element calls for a multilingual and/or multiscriptal turn in WE research, which entails interdisciplinary and transdisciplinary collaborations between scholars from diverse (multilingual) backgrounds. This contribution sheds fresh light on English from an interdisciplinary, multilingual and trans-national perspective.

2 Major Perspectives to Studying English: From Overt and Explicit Use to Covert and Implicit Use

As English has risen to global prominence as the unchallenged *lingua franca* internationally, the all-powerful language has been explored from different perspectives and at different levels over the years. These include approaches that look at (1) the internal dimensions relating to the different grammatical features, properties and aspects of English from within as well as (2) the more external and outward-facing social dimensions concerning English (e.g. English and globalisation). Notably, from the perspective of language contact in particular, there are two main lines of research that have focused on the dominant role of English, which are (1) world Englishes (WE) and (2) the dynamic interactions between English and other less dominant languages (e.g. code-switching and translanguaging).

The first research area involves world Englishes (WE) or regional, localised and indigenised varieties of English from around the world. These include both the outer-circle varieties that are used in former (British) colonies (e.g. India, Sri Lanka, Pakistan, Hong Kong, Singapore, Malaysia, Brunei, the Philippines, Nigeria) and also expanding-circle varieties of English (e.g. Japan, China,

South Korea, Thailand, Poland, Serbia, Italy, France, Russia) that are increasingly used, for example, because of globalisation. Discussions so far in WE research have almost exclusively focused on spoken English as well as English written in the Latin script as people would normally expect. For instance, a user of Indian English may use the phrase 'do the needful' that is archaic and is no longer frequently used in other parts of the English-speaking world. Also, in some South Asian countries, the phrase 'what is your good name' is often heard. In some areas of South(east) Asia and beyond, the expression 'same same but different' is commonly used by salespersons in small businesses.

Another main line of research exploring the powerful nature of English looks at the (dynamic) interactions between English and other local languages. This usually manifests itself in the form of code-mixing, code-switching and/or translanguaging in different educational, professional and sociocultural contexts. This is unsurprising, considering the flexible and open nature of English that is subject to hybridised use (McLellan 2010; Schneider 2016). That is, in an age of globalisation, English, as a dominant linguistic code, is commonly used by language users together with other languages to varying degrees in various scenarios, which results in hybridity and creativity in language usage. For example, a Hindi/Urdu speaker may routinely produce hybridised sentences such as 'Mujhe yeh software bahut pasand hai ... yeh bahut zyada useful aur efficient hai ... honestly yeh bilkul mera favorite hai ... you should use it too ... software try karo, bhai!' (I like this software very much ... it is very useful and efficient ... honestly this is definitely my favourite ... you should use it too ... give the software a try, brother!). Similarly, a Malay-speaker may also mix elements of English to pepper his or her everyday conversation. It is not uncommon in Malaysia to hear sentences like this 'Hey apa khabar? I nak pergi shopping hari ini. Oh by the way, I also heard ada promotion khusus hari ini di food court ... dan minuman adalah percuma ... Oh my God! Jom! Let's go! Jom makan sekarang!' (Hey how are you? I want to go shopping today. Oh by the way, I also heard there is special promotion today in the food court ... and drinks are free ... Oh my God! Come on! Let's go! Let's go eat now!). In the Arabic context, for instance, in the Laish Hip-Hop programme hosted by Big Hass on MIX FM radio station (Saudi Arabia), the host's speaking style features extensive code-switching/translanguaging between Modern Standard Arabic, colloquial Arabic and English. For example, in an episode during the Covid-19 pandemic (11 July 2020 episode), he opened the show by saying the following: 'Assalamualaikum warahmatullahi wabarakatuh [...] ahlan bikum fi halaqa jadeeda [...] wa big up to everybody tuning in [...] aliyoum ... Covid-19 ... Inshallah ... kulna bisahha ... kwayyis ... aham shey ... please wear the masks ... hadha shey jiddan jiddan muhim' (rough translation: Peace be upon you and God's mercy and blessings [...] welcome to you to the new episode [...] and big up to everybody tuning in [...] today ... Covid-19 ... God willing ... all of us are with health ... okay ... the most important thing ... please wear the masks ... this is a very very important thing).

Overall, these two lines of research tend to concern the **more explicit and overt** use of English (e.g. in the spoken form or written in the Latin script) in different settings as a result of language contact. However, an ignored dimension is the **implicit, covert and less obvious manifestations of English** disguised in other less dominant and even 'obscure' and 'exotic' scripts through transliteration. The penetration of English into various non-Latin scripts leads to 'multiscriptal English', giving English a new life and identity in a new environment. While this may well be brushed off as (uninteresting) loan words/borrowings within individual languages, benefiting from documentary multilingual evidence from around the world, we are afforded with a holistic perspective and can make a strong claim of the existence of multiscriptal English. Interdisciplinary, cross-linguistic and transnational in nature, this Element advances scholarship by highlighting an important multilingual and multiscriptal aspect of English, showing how the all-powerful English infiltrates local language(s) surreptitiously.

3 Multiscriptal English Theorised: English Glocalised and Transliterated in Other Languages/Scripts

In our globalised world, there is growing documented evidence to suggest that English often morphs into and even passes off as local languages in local scripts around the world at lexical, phrasal and sentential levels (see the 'I want to travel the world with you' example in Dubai and the 'IT'S A GRIND COFFEE HOUSE' example in Brunei). Such creative and hybridised language use emerging on the ground shows that research on English should not be restricted to the overt and explicit use of English (Roman script) as conventionally assumed. This highlights the need for more attention to exploring English in new ways beyond the traditionally more monolingual and monoscriptal view. Our changing LL calls for novel thinking and conceptualisation in terms of the form English takes in the twenty-first century.

In this Element, the notion 'multiscriptal English' is put forward in some detail, which aptly captures the new transnational, multilingual, multiscriptal and hybridised character (Schneider 2016) English is taking on in a context of change (e.g. increasing language contact in our globalised world). Such a conceptualisation/theorisation represents an important attitudinal change that permits us to explore English in a dynamic, multilingual and multiscriptal way. Without doubt, when English is transliterated and (re)contextualised in different scripts, English takes on multiple manifestations and incarnations. This increasingly common, if not pervasive, linguistic practice injects Anglo-American textures into the existing Semitic, Austronesian, Indo-Aryan, Dravidian or Slavic structures. As such, English gets a new lease of life in the new environment.

The hybridised linguistic practices emerging on the ground also represent a kind of bilingual creativity (cf. Bolton 2002; Kim 2022; Moody and Matsumoto 2003), which is a special kind of creativity which appears in bilingual settings (Takashi Wilkerson 1997). This may lead to bilingual language play (cf. Luk 2013), amongst other things. This is in the sense that speakers who command two languages/scripts may sometimes show agency and transfer patterns of one language into patterns of the other in a creative manner. Clearly, in the case of this Element, sound sequences of English are often transferred into various local languages/scripts, hence a manifestation of bilingual creativity. Such bilingual creativity may only be understood and appreciated by people with certain knowledge of English and another language/script (e.g. English and Arabic or English and Russian).

In the transliteration and (re)contextualisation process, English words, phrases and even sentences are inevitably rendered based on the transliteraters' (individual) understandings of English pronunciation. Also, the process is conditioned and shaped by the affordances/repertoires/constraints of the local scripts and languages. As we shall see later, transliterating English is easier in some languages/scripts than others. That is, due to differences between various writing and sound systems, precise correspondence often is not easy. For example, as will be discussed in more details, the 'p' and 'g' sounds do not exist in the standard Arabic writing system. As such, adjustments are needed in the conversion process. Similarly, in rendering English sounds into Korean, certain elements (e.g. vowels) may need to be added to conform to rules/preferences in the target system.

The transliterated language from English represents a relatively new beast, which takes on new flavours after the inter-scriptal transliteration process. English (re)contextualised into a local script represents the interface or borderlands between the two languages, thus bridging traditionally distant, if not diametrically different, languages. This also gives rise to new hybridised identities in both languages as the resulting transliterated language may be viewed as simultaneously containing both familiar and foreign elements by speakers of the two languages. The transliteration of English into local scripts leads to a localisation of English. This also leads to an Englishisation (cf.

Kachru 1994) or Anglicisation of the local linguistic landscape as a result. Clearly, in the making of multiscriptal English, English is the content-exporting language, representing the starting point of creative language use in other languages/scripts. Arguably, at the beginning, multiscriptal English in local scripts may be symbolic and even decorative (cf. Gu and Almanna 2023; Phanthaphoommee and Gu 2024) in nature and has limited informational value. Over time, multiscriptal English may become taken for granted and entrenched in the host language. That is, once indigenised and enshrined in the local scripts in the written form and become widely visible in the LL, English at different levels may be more easily incorporated, absorbed and consolidated as part of the local languages in a surreptitious manner. As such, English, at a macro level, may be seen as a kind of 'meaning potential' that can be unleashed and activated. The all-powerful English, as the content-exporting language, possesses the potentiality to become part of other languages and effect far-reaching changes to those languages/scripts at the receiving end over time (at lexical, phrasal and even sentential levels). Once established, consolidated and taken for granted as a common and effortless practice that is cool and trendy by certain businesses/actors, this cumulatively may lead to further imitation and copycat behaviours by other businesses/actors. Indeed, the phenomenon of transliterating English into local script is becoming increasingly visible in the Middle East (e.g. Dubai and Doha) and elsewhere, compared with a few decades ago. This is particularly true given the fact that LLs mould the lives of a place's inhabitants, business owners and even sign-makers who are surrounded and shaped by countless signage (Alomoush and Al-Naimat 2020) on a daily basis. The frequent use of the strategy may give local languages new hybridised identities and bring about new realities. If used excessively, it also remains to be seen whether the local cultural and linguistic heritage of those languages at the receiving end might be affected or eschewed over time.

4 Multiscriptal English, Translanguaging, Multilingualism and Lexical Borrowing

Having conceptualised 'multiscriptal English', the relationships between 'multiscriptal English', translanguaging, multilingualism and lexical borrowing are explored here. Arguably, all of these concepts involve some degrees of border-crossing, hybridity or co-existence of different language systems. However, multilingualism is a rather generic term with different aspects and realisations. Given the different languages/scripts involved, translanguaging and 'multiscriptal English' have some overlaps with the general idea of 'multilingualism'. As a relatively recent yet popular concept, 'translanguaging' may be understood in various ways with different manifestations. However, in general, translanguaging concerns the ability to fluidly move between different languages, where language users activate and utilise their multilingual and multimodal repertoires (García and Li 2014) dynamically. It is also a pedagogical approach applicable to language teaching and education in general, especially in diverse multilingual contexts. The role of translanguaging can be conceptual, theoretical, descriptive and methodological and pedagogical (García and Li 2014; Li 2018). Given the wide-ranging use of the term, it is not always easy to say what translanguaging is. To some, it provides a useful analytical/descriptive lens to help explain certain linguistic phenomena and linguistic practices (e.g. code-switching and other dynamic, creative and hybridised language use). To some, translanguaging is an empowering and liberal pedagogical approach, a liberating ideological perspective, and even a decolonizing project (Li and García 2022), aimed at moving beyond named languages and countering the monolingual ideology and the prevailing understandings of multilingualism in education and beyond.

'Multiscriptal English' has some similarities with translanguaging since multiscriptal English also represents a fusion and hybridity (cf. Schneider 2016) and is a relatively novel variety that goes beyond named languages. However, compared with the seemingly wide-ranging and 'all-encompassing' nature of 'translanguaging' and 'multilingualism', 'multiscriptal English', despite its hybridised property, is more narrow and is arguably a more specific and radical phenomenon that has emerged in recent decades. While translanguaging and multilingualism in practice can involve different languages/language combinations in a dynamic and fluid way, 'multiscriptal English' involves mostly the one-way importation and (often wholesale) transliteration of English into less dominant languages/scripts phonetically, given the imbalanced and lopsided nature of different languages in our world as a linguistic market (Bourdieu 1977). Also, while translanguaging and multilingualism in general can involve different modes of communication and may have important pedagogical components, multiscriptal English is mostly to do with the written form (e.g. written signs in shopfronts, business names and advertisements in different non-Latin scripts) and is more conceptual, descriptive and analytical in nature. The concept serves to capture this increasingly visible phenomenon witnessed in multiple scripts/languages globally (e.g. India, Pakistan, South Korea, Thailand, Brunei, the UAE, Qatar and Saudi Arabia), due to globalisation and language contact.

Also, 'multiscriptal English' explored here has some overlap with and is not contradictory to the well-researched concept of 'lexical borrowing'. To some extent, lexical borrowing is a precursor of the phenomenon under discussion here. That is, there is parallelism of the results of lexical borrowing into local scripts and the outcomes of multiscriptal English explored in this Element. As such, when English words are phonetically transliterated into indigenous languages/scripts, their English origins remain obscure. However, although from a result-oriented perspective, multiscriptal English looks like lexical borrowing (from English), there are also significant differences between them, especially as far as the reasons or motivations are concerned. Notably, 'lexical borrowing' is often to bridge certain lexical-conceptual gaps between different languages. In other words, these are often to do with lexical items or concepts that are not easily translatable. However, while the boundary may occasionally be fuzzy, the idea of 'multiscriptal English' points to an increasingly common phenomenon for elements of English (e.g. words, phrases, expressions and sentences) to be phonetically rendered into local scripts not necessarily due to necessity (e.g. lexical gaps) but for certain stylistic, commercial, branding, and/or ideological purposes and to create certain images (e.g. modern, fashionable, cool, sophisticated and international). This is largely from the powerful language English into other less dominant languages/scripts. As illustrated in this Element, multiscriptal English comes alive, when names such as 'BLACK & BLUE', 'Happy Land Corner', 'Day to Day', 'The Face Shop', 'Star Family Meal', 'Penny Fashion', 'Quality Foods', 'Rest and Relax', 'IT'S A GREAT COFFEE HOUSE' are phonetically rendered into different languages/scripts.

5 Linguistic Landscape (LL) as Theoretical Framework, Methodology and Vivid Site to Studying Evolving English in Action

Signs are everywhere in our linguistic landscape yet they sometimes escape our attention, despite their important indexical values and social meanings. While 'linguistic landscape' as a concept and fact is technically at least as old as written language (Kallen 2023), LL research in the modern sense is relatively new. This section explores linguistic landscape (LL) as both a framework and methodology and also a vital site to investigating the constantly evolving language use in our dynamic world. Against a backdrop of globalisation and (super)diversity and thanks to the advent of digital photography (Gorter 2006) and other technological tools, linguistic landscape (LL) has gradually consolidated itself as a rapidly maturing and increasingly vital field (cf. Landry and Bourhis 1997; Spolsky and Cooper 1991) related to multilingualism, (socio)linguistics, applied linguistics and so on. Of an interdisciplinary orientation and drawing on real-life linguistic data, LL is attentive to documenting, describing and analysing authentic and naturally occurring language use in a range of sociopolitical, institutional and cultural contexts (Coluzzi

2016; Gu and Almanna 2023; Kallen 2023; Landry and Bourhis 1997; Scollon and Scollon 2003).

According to a classic definition provided by Landry and Bourhis (1997: 23), LL research focuses on the 'visibility and salience of languages' on both monolingual and multilingual signage. These can be signs enacted and emplaced in various forms and formats (e.g. street signs, public notices, posters, advertisements, shop and restaurant signage, commercial billboards and even murals and graffiti). The focus on signs provides interesting insights into multilingualism and language in general, permitting a detailed look at different aspects of language use (e.g. script use, font size, calligraphic style, colour, what languages are foregrounded and backgrounded, and the power relations between different linguistic codes) and the potential reasons behind certain linguistic phenomena.

Our urban space, both socially shaped and socially shaping, may be understood as a sociosymbolic text and a narrative (Gu and Almanna 2023) or a discourse. This points to the socially constructed and mediated nature of our dynamic, complex and superdiverse cityscapes. A place's LL represents a 'gestalt' (Ben-Rafael 2009), which can be understood as a collection of multi-semiotic, multimodal, multi-authored and multi-layered texts. A place's LL mirrors and sheds light on its language policies, language ideologies and attitudes, ethnolinguistic vitality, power relations and also a place's historical background and demographic and sociolinguistic profiles. Therefore, a place's cityscape or urban linguistic landscape may be 'read', analysed and interpreted, which provides a vital entry point or entrée into various aspects and dimensions of our dynamic, multifaceted and multilingual societies.

There are top-down and bottom-up signs (Ben-Rafael et al. 2006). Top-down signs are formal or official signs made and instituted by various governments, institutions and different bodies and agencies. In comparison, bottom-up signs are less formal in nature, which refer to signs designed and emplaced by non-official bodies and communities, small businesses and individuals at a grass-roots level. While top-down signage often mirrors the official language ideology and policy, bottom-up signs are more diversified and dynamic, reflecting a locale's sociolinguistic and ethnolinguistic situations on the ground (Gu 2023a). Indeed, private and non-official signs at a bottom-up level are the best artefacts (Huebner 2006), because they are poised to reveal inhabitants' underlying language attitudes, ideologies and preferences in a salient way. Within individual multilingual signs and also at a neighbourhood level, LL can be viewed as the space where translanguaging and other hybridised language practices are instantiated and the LL itself in many ways represents a multilingual and multimodal repertoire (Gorter and Cenoz 2015) in our increasingly dynamic and complex societies. The presence (or absence) of language displays in our society, for Shohamy (2006), can convey multiple important messages. This can not only be indexical of but also can have broader ramifications on various socioeconomic, political and cultural aspects of our societies. LL research intersects with such related subjects and topics as sociolinguistics, applied linguistics, (multimodal) discourse analysis, semiotics, translation studies, language planning and policy, world Englishes, anthropology, area studies, multilingual and intercultural communication, urban studies, tourism studies, business and marketing, history, ethnography, sociology, demographics, and even geography. Since multiple phenomena and issues may manifest themselves on our LL in multifarious ways, LL is far from being a monolithic approach. LL can be explored from a range of perspectives, depending on the specific issue under investigation and the location being studied.

After about two decades' development, scholars have explored LLs in an array of geographical, sociopolitical, cultural, commercial and institutional contexts and settings (Blommaert 2013; Lai 2013; Lam 2023; Lee 2022; Spolsky and Cooper 1991) in our (increasingly) diverse, multicultural, and multilingual societies in both the global north (cf. Blackwood and Tufi 2015; Lim and Perono Cacciafoco 2023; Lou 2016) and more recently also the global south (cf. Gallagher and Bataineh 2020; Gu and Almanna 2023; Gu 2024a; 2024b; McKiernan 2021; Troyer 2012; Taylor-Leech 2012). Despite their multifarious foci, these empirical LL studies have pointed to how looking at naturally occurring signs may usefully reveal and help index the other linguistic, sociocultural (Theng and Lee 2022), economic, institutional, political, demographic (Gu 2023a), ideological, religious (Coluzzi 2022; Spolsky and Cooper 1991), and even public health communication (Gu 2023b; 2023c; Lees 2021) dimensions of our increasingly diverse and complex (urban) spaces (Amos 2016; Hopkyns and van den Hoven 2022; Huebner 2006) beyond the signs per se. And what unites linguistic landscape studies together is arguably the data-driven, descriptivist and socially engaged approach to authentic language use enacted in our spaces.

Undergirding these extant LL studies, a major line of inquiry concerns how English figures prominently or is increasingly visible in different locales (cf. Alomoush 2019; Piller 2003). That is, English's role and dominance represent an important part of LL research to date. Indeed, Bolton (2012) and Bolton, Botha and Lee (2020) have made a case for the close nexus between linguistic landscape (LL) and world Englishes (WE) research. Linguistic landscape, in many ways, represents a site *par excellence* to closely and critically examine how English is used for various purposes in different contexts.

Of a growing body of LL studies exploring the prominence of English, Tang (2020) and Zhang, Tupas and Norhaida (2020) have pointed to the dominance of English in multilingual Singapore. Despite the fact that the four official languages Malay, Mandarin, Tamil and English supposedly should enjoy equal status, there is in reality a pecking order and English predominates. Even Singapore's Chinatown is English-dominated (Zhang, Tupas, and Norhaida 2020). McKiernan (2021) explores English in a Malaysian border town's LL. Coluzzi (2016) looks at Brunei's LL, examining the visibility and prestige of English. Also, Manan et al. (2017) studied the prominence/pervasiveness of English in Pakistan's LL (in Quetta). Focusing on Covid-related LL in the UAE, Hopkyns and van den Hoven (2022) and Gu (2023c) point to the prominence of English (alongside Arabic) at the expense of other minority and/or migrant languages. Similarly, Gu and Almanna (2023) and Ahmed (2020) point towards the dominance of English in the linguistic/semiotic landscape of Dubai and the UAE.

Beyond the LLs of outer-circle post-colonial societies or places heavily influenced by the British Empire, English is also visible in expanding-circle countries and regions around the world. Against a backdrop of neoliberal globalisation, Manan and Hajar (2022) zoomed in on the role of English on the LL of Nur-Sultan, capital of Kazakhstan. An & Zhang (2022), Yuan (2019), Xiao & Lee (2022), Liu & Ma (2023), Li (2015), and Yan (2023) point to the growing presence of English in mainland China in multiple cities. Similarly, English in Japan's LL is examined by Rowland (2016). Troyer (2012) studied English in Thailand's linguistic netscape. Foster & Welsh (2021) explored English usage in Indonesia. Lin (2023) examined English in Cambodia's LL as a result of globalisation and tourism. Also, Bruyèl-Olmedo & Juan-Garau (2020) looked at English in Spain, exploring the linguistic landscapes of two tourist resorts. Nikolaou (2017) highlighted the visibility of English in the LL of Athens. Attentive to the situation in Ecuador, Lavender (2020) looks into English's role in the LL of Azogues. Focusing on Africa's LL, Lanza & Woldemariam (2014) explored English as an index of modernity.

These studies contribute to our understanding of English's role in our globalised world, pointing towards colonialism, postcolonialism, globalisation, neoliberalism, consumerism and tourism as main drivers behind English's visibility globally. However, despite their merits, almost all of these studies only examined written English in the conventional and taken-for-granted Latin script (the explicit and overt manifestations of English). These LL studies therefore have implicitly made the assumption that English only appears in/can only be studied in the traditional form (e.g. the Latin script). Using LL as a theoretical framework, method and a site of empirical data (or a corpus), this study reveals the hidden, covert and underexplored side of English that is camouflaged in different locales' LLs in a seemingly innocuous way. That is, English is increasingly transliterated into other scripts/languages, thus leading to a novel variety called multiscriptal English.

6 The Translational and Cross-Linguistic Aspect of the Making of (Multilingual) Linguistic Landscapes

Despite translation's centrality (Simon 2012) in the making of multilingual and multicultural urban spaces (Cronin 2006), the translational and cross-linguistic aspects have been significantly underexplored in LL research to date. Only recently, the nexus between LL and translation has been explored by a few researchers. Focusing on Kazan in Russia, Aristova's (2016) LL study uses English translations as a marker to explore the making of an emerging global city. Koskinen (2014) examined the translational/multilingual practices evidenced in Finnish city Tampere's LL. Song (2020; 2023) examined Hong Kong and Macau's LLs from a translational perspective. Focusing on Covidscapes (Covid-related LLs), Gu (2023b; 2023c) investigated translation and multilingual communication in global cities like Hong Kong at a time of a pandemic. Focusing on the Greek context, Lees (2021) explored LL from the perspective of translation. Looking at the translation and multilingual practices, Lee (2022) highlights the choreographed nature of Singapore's LL. Gu and Almanna (2023) explored the Arabic-English pair, pointing to the fact that the all-powerful English is often transliterated into Arabic in Dubai's LL. Piller (2018) and Manan et al. (2017) shed some interesting light on the translational aspects, alluding to the use of transliteration as a phenomenon in Dubai and Pakistan's LLs respectively.

Despite the small number, these studies point to the importance of exploring the translational and cross-linguistic aspects of our urban LLs. Through comparative and cross-linguistic analysis, we can develop a deeper knowledge of the translational relationship between different languages on signage. This permits us to gain insights into the power relations between different linguistic codes (e.g. information is translated from which language into which language, what information is foregrounded or backgrounded, what rendering strategies are adopted). Since power and ideology are often the most salient when their workings are least visible (cf. Fairclough 1989), the phenomenon under discussion here is of interest in helping inform the power and dominance of English (Pennycook 2010) in our (post)colonial and globalised world.

7 Multiscriptal English in Action: Evidence from Multiple Languages and Scripts around the World

Rather than focusing on one locale, this Element presents documented evidence from multiple languages/scripts around the world to illustrate multiscriptal English in action, that is, English being transliterated into local scripts and even passing off as local languages in our globalised world. The phenomenon described here results from over ten years' close observations (2011–2024) based on the author's experience studying, working, researching, visiting and travelling in different parts of the world. Some of the world's major non-Roman scripts are covered (e.g. the Devanagari script, the Thai script, the Cyrillic script, the Korean alphabet, the Japanese writing system, the Arabic script and various Arabic-based scripts such as Jawi and the Urdu script). This permits the author to approach the topic from a transnational, multilingual and multiscriptal perspective.

Methodologically, a walking ethnography approach was taken, which is common in linguistic landscape research. Since the author has familiarity with certain writing systems (e.g. the Russian alphabet, the Korean alphabet and various Arabic-derived systems for example for writing Arabic, Urdu and Malay), examples of 'multiscriptal English' could be easily identified for these languages. Over time, the author developed a good sense and intuition in terms of what kinds of texts (in which contexts) are likely to feature this phenomenon.

For other writing systems the author is less familiar with (e.g. Thai and Tamil), based on intuition and previous experience, the author was able to take photographs of cases that were likely to feature this transliterated use of language (e.g. in high-profile shopping malls and other businesses in urban spaces). This is based on the commonsensical belief and assumption that this phenomenon is likely to be more commonly found in commercialised urban areas than remote places less influenced by globalisation and a market-driven neoliberal ideology (e.g. small towns or villages). The photographed images were then checked through putting the texts into translation software such as Google translate to confirm whether or not the versions, for instance, in Thai and Tamil were transliterated from English.

After the data collection and checking processes, the author has access to a multilingual/multiscriptal corpus that features this phenomenon (898 photographs in Arabic, 289 photographs in Urdu, 195 photographs of Malay in the Jawi script, 121 photographs in Nepali, 311 photographs in Thai, 136 photographs in Russian, 183 photographs in Korean, 198 photographs in Japanese, 66 photographs in Tamil, 73 photographs in Bengali, 87 photographs in Chinese). In most cases, it is very clear and straightforward that the powerful code English is transliterated into local languages/scripts (e.g. Mr. D.I.Y., UPANDRUNNING, Star Family Meal, The Cheesecake Factory, LADS BURGER, MILLIONAIRE HAIR STYLE, Beauty World, City Walk) partially or in its entirety. Internationalisms, place names and/or brand names (e.g. NIKE, ADIDAS and iPhone) that often cannot otherwise be translated semantically are not included in the corpus (even though these cases may still be related to the idea of 'multiscriptal English' to some extent). Also, names that are clearly not English in origin (e.g. Daiso and Mixue) are similarly not included (even though to the uninitiated and general customers these might be taken for granted as English in a globalised world). Notably, however, brand/product names such as 'Superdry', 'Burger King', 'Pepper Lunch', 'Forever 21' and 'FIVE GUYS' are included in the corpus as these names can technically be semantically rendered into different languages (that is, transliteration, if used, is a stylistic preference and conscious ideological choice and not a necessity). In exceptional cases, the researcher's discretion and academic judgement were used (which inevitably are needed in most studies in the humanities and social sciences).

Proportionate to the author's varying degrees of proficiency in these languages/scripts, understandably, a differentiated approach is taken in the analysis/discussion section. For certain languages, attempts are made to shed light on the inter-scriptal transliteration process (e.g. any sounds added or omitted and any shifts). In other cases, the author can only demonstrate the presence/existence of English disguised in certain scripts. At any rate, this Element only serves as an important starting point for scholars to show more attentiveness to this interesting phenomenon. In so doing, more interdisciplinary future studies can systematically explore the internal mechanisms and workings of the inter-scriptal and cross-lingual transliteration process and the making of multiscriptal English.

In discussing examples of multiscriptal English in different scripts, it is important to offer readers an idea of how the resulting multiscriptal English words/phrases sound like for better understanding. A phonetic notation system like IPA may seem useful. However, despite its seemingly sophisticated and systematic nature, the IPA system has its weaknesses. Also, the IPA system is too precise and seemingly pins things down to fixed textbook-style pronunciations in a prescriptive way. However, in reality, the picture is more complicated. That is, how these multiscriptal English words/phrases are pronounced is often open to interpretation. Given the transliterated/mediated nature of multiscriptal English, it is often not precise or fixed in pronunciation. There is often a degree of fuzziness because the transliterator inevitably transliterates based on his or her own understandings of the two writing systems involved. Once a transliterated version is created, it too is not fixed and is subject to different understandings and dynamic interpretations by those reading the signs based on their own dialects/accents. For example, for جراند (transliterated from 'grand'), many Arabic speakers may pronounce it like 'jrand' ('j' as in 'junk') yet speakers of Egyptian Arabic are likely to pronounce it like 'grand' (hard 'g'). This is because ج in Standard Arabic and many dialects is pronounced as 'j', yet it is pronounced like a hard 'g' (voiced velar plosive) by some Egyptians and Yemenis. Similarly, the 'r' sound in Malay (corresponding to ر in the Arabic-based Jawi script) is pronounced differently in different Malay dialects in Malaysia and other parts of the Malay world (e.g. Brunei and Indonesia). Therefore, pinning things down to fixed pronunciations using IPA or similar systems risks being too precise and thus imprecise. To solve this issue, in many languages covered (e.g. Arabic, Urdu, Malay in the Jawi script, Russian, Japanese), the researcher decided to only provide rough pronunciations of multiscriptal English words/phrases to give an idea of how they 'literally' sound in a basic yet hopefully sufficient way to get the point across (this also allows for a degree of fuzziness). For languages such as Thai and Tamil (which the author is less familiar with), the approximate pronunciations enabled by Google translate are used to give a rough idea of the pronunciation after the inter-scriptal conversion. Given the differences between these languages (e.g. Thai and Tamil) and English and the lack of a universal transliteration convention, using the rough pronunciations enabled by Google translate, however imperfect, is deemed sufficient for illustrative purposes and permits a degree of replicability.

Given the illustrative nature of the following case studies, it is beyond the scope of this Element to systematically pin down a number and say the phenomenon accounts for what percent in each country/place definitively (this is also impossible to achieve given various practical constraints and challenges). However, some scholars have attempted to provide some statistical information (cf. Gu and Almanna 2023; Manan et al. 2017; Mahmood et al. 2021). According to Gu and Almanna's (2023) study, in Dubai, approximately 55 per cent of signs investigated feature English disguised in the Arabic script. For the places explored in this Element, as a general estimate, the phenomenon may account for anywhere between 10 per cent and 70 per cent in business and shop signs (which is particularly visible in the UAE, Brunei and central Bangkok and also in the Korean context).

As explored in more details below, English is widely transliterated into local languages/scripts, thus leading to 'multiscriptal English'. The making of multi-scriptal English constitutes a glocalisation/recontextualisation process. Given the differences between various writing systems, adaptions/adjustments are often needed to meet the rules/preferences of the target writing systems.

There is often no fixed approach in glocalising and recontextualising English into various local languages/scripts. This can be highly individualistic and even idiosyncratic, depending on the transliterater's personalised understandings of the English pronunciation and the local language's orthography and affordances.

7.1 The UAE, Qatar and the Gulf Region

With strategic location at the intersection of Asia, Europe and Africa, the gulf region has since ancient times been the meeting point of different languages, peoples, ideas and religions (Piller 2018). Over time, Islam became the dominant religion and Arabic became established as the dominant language. For centuries, the living conditions in the Gulf had remained relatively basic partly due to the harsh and barren natural environments. In more recent history, most states in the region (e.g. the UAE, Qatar, Oman, Kuwait, Bahrain) were to varying degrees under the influences of the British Empire. Several decades ago, these Gulf countries gained independence from the British. Thanks to the discovery of oil, the vision of the political leaders, and large-scale arrival of (temporary) migrant workers (e.g. from India, Pakistan, Nepal, Bangladesh and Sri Lanka and also Southeast Asian countries such as the Philippines and Indonesia), many Gulf states have risen to global prominence and become rich economies (Siemund and Leimgruber 2020). The rapid development of the region has given rise to a few global cities of superlatives (Gu and Song 2024; Piller 2018). Dubai in the UAE is but one vivid exemplum of the region's recent success story and meteoric rise. With the mass transnational movement of people, now in many countries in the region (e.g. Qatar and the UAE), the local Arabic-speaking natives are often outnumbered (Gu 2023a; Gu and Almanna 2023) by foreign workers from diverse sociolinguistic, cultural and religious backgrounds (Ahmad and Hillman 2021; Hopkyns and van den Hoven 2022). These foreign workers are normally employed on a non-permanent basis without further pathway to citizenship. The Gulf represents a region of great superdiversity (Blommaert 2013; Piller 2018; Vertovec 2007) in the twenty-first century. However, such superdiversity does not easily translate into a melting pot. Expats from different groups tend to socialise amongst themselves (Walsh 2006), which results in multiple parallel worlds in the same society.

In terms of language, Arabic is often an official language as a reflection of the region's Islamic heritage and Arabic traditions. English is also an important language in sectors such as business, commerce and education. English effectively serves as a de facto lingua franca which facilitates communication between people from diverse backgrounds (Ahmed 2020; Gu and Almanna 2023). Additionally, other migrants' languages (e.g. Hindi, Urdu, Punjabi, Nepali, Malayalam, Tamil, Bengali, Tagalog, Indonesian, Chinese) can also be heard in the region's soundscape. Overall, the (written) linguistic landscapes in the Gulf are dominated by Arabic and English (Ahmad and Hillman 2021; Gu 2023c).

While the phenomenon of transliterating information from the Latin script (e.g. English or French) into the Arabic script can be seen in the Middle East and Northern Africa (MENA) region in general, such a linguistic practice seemingly is particularly pervasive in the Gulf region (e.g. the UAE, Oman, Qatar, Bahrain, Kuwait, Saudi Arabia). This may be attributable to the fact that the Gulf countries are more international and diverse and are more implicated in the broader trends of globalisation, consumerism and neoliberalism (cf. Piller 2018). For illustrative purposes, examples of such practices in the UAE (Dubai and Abu Dhabi) and also Qatar (Doha) are presented and discussed. In Arabic, sometimes, vowels are not explicitly written. For example, نحن means 'we' in standard Arabic and is pronounced 'nahnu'. Yet, if we look at what is written alone, it reads 'nhn' (vowels are not clearly indicated). In Arabic, diacritical marks can be added to help better indicate the pronunciation. However, diacritical marks are often not written. Due to exposure to and familiarity with the language, native Arabic speakers can usually figure out different words. However, as far as English transliterated into the Arabic script is concerned, since it is not authentic language taken for granted by native speakers, vowels tend to be more explicitly indicated so that the transliterated language is more 'spelled out'. As seen in examples later, the elements in Arabic and English can be arranged in a few different ways. These notably include Arabic texts being placed above English (see first two signs in Figure 1 for example). Also, it is common to see Arabic being placed on the right-hand side and English text being placed on the left-hand side (see the last sign in Figure 1 as one example out of many). Notably, all Arabic words are written from right to left in any sign (English is normally written from left to right). This structure is illustrated in Figure 17.

7.1.1 The UAE (Dubai and Abu Dhabi)

The UAE (United Arab Emirates) gained independence in 1971 after an extended period of Britain's (colonial) influences in the region. Despite its humble beginnings and harsh climate, the UAE has risen to global prominence in recent decades. As with other countries in the region, Arabic and English are widely seen in the linguistic landscape in the UAE including the superdiverse

Figure 1 Signs featuring English and English transliterated into the Arabic script

global cities Dubai and Abu Dhabi (Ahmed 2020; Piller 2018). The glocalisation of English into the Arabic script is highly prominent in Dubai, a glitzy poster child of the region. In Figure 1, there are 8 'bilingual' signs in Arabic and English. Arabic in all of these involves full or partial transliteration from the information in English. In the first sign, DUBAI MALL FOUNTAIN VIEWS is rendered into Arabic as 'dbii muul fauntn fiuz'. The Arabic version may not make sense were it not placed next to the corresponding English version. Notably, in the second sign, THE PALM MONORAIL is a major public transportation project in Dubai, which takes passengers to the iconic Palm Jumeirah. On the transportation system's website, the Palm Monorail is described as 'the most iconic way to navigate across the Palm Jumeirah', which is 'not a mere form of transportation' but 'an experiential journey to explore astonishing landmarks with every stop' (https://www.palmmonorail.com/). Despite being a more formal and public-facing top-down sign, the Arabic information represents a wholesale transliteration of the name in English, rather than using real and pure Arabic. For example, 'palm' is a common kind of tree in Dubai and the broader Gulf region. In authentic Arabic, نخيل (nkhiil) is the common name for palm trees. However, the English word 'palm' is transliterated into the Arabic script instead as 'balm'. In the Arabic version of the name, even the definite article 'the' is phonetically rendered into 'Arabic' as 'اذ' (dha). The use of transliteration arguably is from a commercial and branding perspective, giving the project a global and international identity. In the third sign about the CITY WALK project, clearly, the Arabic name (which reads 'siitii waaok') is also directly transliterated from English, despite the obvious existence of lexical items in pure Arabic. This strategy is also seemingly driven and motivated by marketing and branding considerations. In the fourth sign, Fabyland is a children's amusement centre in the area of Dubai Festival City (دبي فستيفال سيتي), a major and high-profile business, entertainment and residential development in Dubai. Clearly, the Arabic name (which reads 'fabiland') is a direct transliteration of the English name 'Fabyland'. Also, even the local 'Arabic' name ('dbii fstiifaal siitii') of the broader project/development itself is transliterated from the English version 'Dubai Festival City'. Similarly, this strategy is also fully or partially used in the following two signs featuring the 'catch 22' restaurant and the 'GULF COURT HOTEL BUSINESS BAY'. While these examples largely concern project or business names (e.g. nouns), the last two signs are more salient, interesting and radical examples of the observed phenomenon. As illustrated in Figure 1 (penultimate sign), this is a Pandora advertisement spotted in a brochure in Dubai. What is fascinating is that the whole 'Arabic' sentence 'آي وونت تو ترافل ذي وورلد ويذ يو' (ai wont tu traafl dhi world widh yu) turns out to be a transliteration of the English counterpart 'I want to travel the world with you'. It is unclear why this strategy is adopted as opposed to using proper and authentic Arabic. The sentence can be easily rendered into modern standard Arabic semantically as 'أريد السفر حول العالم معك'. The last example in this figure was found outside a high-end salon catering to men in the CITY WALK area. This example also features a long unit made up of several English words (Executive Grooming For Men) being transliterated into Arabic. These examples beg the question as to whether this strategy of rendering sounds by means of Arabic letters really works as far as effective real communication is concerned. However, since English is the dominant language in marketing and business, presumably, transliterating English into local Arabic script may be considered cool, posh and marketable by the sign-maker, in a globalized, neoliberal and consumeristic context. This sign as well as the other signs analysed before point towards the all-powerful nature of English in Dubai so much so that even information in English is transliterated into Arabic using the Arabic script at phrasal/sentential levels at the expense of rendering the actual meanings.

The aforementioned examples involving the strategy of transliterating English into Arabic are far from being isolated and cherry-picked cases. This phenomenon is rather widespread in Dubai and the UAE in general. Sometimes, even on supposedly information-heavy road signs, most information may extensively feature transliterated Arabic (from English). The example in Figure 2 is a publicly displayed three-way signpost found in the popular and high-end Dubai Marina area. Essentially the phonetically corresponding elements in Arabic and English versions are underlined in red. As can be seen in the Figure, around 80 per cent of the 'Arabic' words are not pure Arabic but are direct phonetic transliterations from their English counterparts. For example, Dubai Marina Mall's local Arabic version is simply 'دبي مارينا مول' (dbii mariina mawl). Other examples include Trident Bayside, Marina Diamond, Dubai

Figure 2 A three-way signpost in the Dubai Marina area

Marina Towers and Marriott Harbour. This strategy is employed despite the existence of pure Arabic words for 'diamond', 'tower', 'harbour' and so on. This is just one representative example (out of many), which vividly suggests that in Dubai Arabic may often play second fiddle in the face of the more powerful code English.

The publicly displayed sign (Figure 3) found in Dubai's popular and expat-friendly Jumeirah Beach Residence (JBR) area is another salient example. The elements in Arabic and English featuring essentially the same messages (phonetically) are highlighted in red. For example, the English names 'THE BEACH SOUTH' and 'Bla Bla Beach Club' are phonetically rendered simply as 'dha biitsh saoth' and 'bla bla biitsh klub' in the Arabic script respectively. Statistically, approximately 95 per cent of all the 'Arabic' words in this sign are transliterations from the English versions. This constitutes a highly mechanical way of communication, where sound is obviously prioritised

Figure 3 Signpost in Jumeirah Beach Residence area

at the expense of meaning. The communication practice can be potentially explained by a myriad of factors including the place's (semi)colonial history, the juggernaut of English, the recent trend of globalisation, the neoliberal ideology and market forces, language contact and the snob value of writing English in the Arabic script.

Notably, given the vast differences between the Arabic and English writing systems, various changes and transformations may take place in the transliteration process. It is not uncommon to see that certain English sounds cannot be directly rendered using the Arabic script. As such, certain inter-scriptal adaptations need to be made. Also, there is often no fixed way of rendering English into Arabic. The transliteration process is sometimes done in a discretionary and random manner, which may exhibit the sign-author's individual style and personalised understanding of English pronunciation.

To explain, let us have a look at the signs in Figure 4. In the first sign, the English name of the business 'Golden Valley' in Dubai is phonetically represented as 'jooldn faali' in Arabic. Clearly, due to the major differences between the two systems, a number of transformations can be found when English is recontextualised into the Arabic script. For example, the 'g' sound in English is represented as a 'j' sound (ج) in the Arabic script due to the fact that the 'g' sound often does not exist in the Arabic writing system (interestingly in the

Figure 4 Signs in Dubai

Egyptian dialect of Arabic, the letter ج sounds like 'g'). Also, the 'v' sound often cannot be represented using the Arabic script. As such, transliteraters will have to use other letters in the Arabic script in order to (re)create the 'v' sound. In this case, ف ('f') is used. As such, 'valley' becomes 'faali' in the Arabic version. In the second example in Figure 4, the brand name 'THE BODY SHOP' is rendered into Arabic as ذي بودي شوب [dhi boodi shoob]. Clearly, the 'p' sound in English as in 'shop' is transliterated as a 'b' sound (ب) in Arabic due to the fact that in the Arabic script the 'p' sound does not exist. In the next example, the name 'GUESS' is transliterated into the Arabic script as جس (js). As discussed earlier, the 'g' sound often does not exist in the Arabic script, the 'j' sound is used instead. Also, as vowels are not clearly indicated, it is not straightforward to know how the Arabic version should be pronounced exactly (for example whether it should be jis, jos, jes or joos). In the last example, the corresponding Arabic name for 'BURJ VISTA' is rendered as 'brj fiista'. While the word 'burj' is transliterated from Arabic, the word 'fiista' in the Arabic script is phonetically rendered from 'vista'. Again, due to a lack of corresponding sound, 'v' as in 'vista' is represented as 'f' in the Arabic version. Notably, while sometimes Arabic is placed above English and sometimes below English, in many signs (Figure 4 and elsewhere), the English information tends to be placed on the left-hand side (where English is read from left to right) and the Arabic information (phonetically transliterated from English) is placed on the right-hand side (the Arabic information is read from right to left). This leads to a parallel design (the red arrows in Figure 4 indicate text orientations for both languages). Please see Figure 17 for detailed illustration.

Figure 5 showcases more examples of the trend where the 'Arabic' versions tend to be transliterated from their English counterparts (in a wholesale manner). Notably, in the first sign, 'LET'S GO' is represented as 'liits qoo'. In other words, the 'g' sound in 'go' is realised as ق ('q') using the letter qaf. While this letter is pronounced like a 'q' in standard Arabic, it is worth mentioning that in some gulf Arabic dialects, the letter sounds like 'g'. Therefore, to some gulf Arabic speakers, such a transliteration does sound like 'go' in English. Since this sign is found in Dubai, such a transliteration makes sense. However, interestingly, even in the same city, which is Dubai, different Arabic letters (e.g. ج, ق and غ) are used to represent the 'g' sound in English (which does not exist in standard Arabic). We can see that in the second and third sign in this figure, both of them also involve the English word 'go', that is, 'STOP&GO' and 'PHONE TO GO'. However, the same word is represented differently in the two shops: one is represented as جو (jo) and the other one as غو 'gho'. This points to the fact that transliterating English into Arabic can be highly individualised and even idiosyncratic, where transliteraters have different

Figure 5 Signs in Dubai

understandings of the pronunciations of words and may use the target scripts differently. Such inconsistencies make English written in the Arabic script difficult to recognise and understand. In the fifth sign, the English name of the business is 'SEVEN GOLDEN GATES'. Yet, this is rendered as 'sfn joldn jiits' in the Arabic script due to the fact that certain sounds (e.g. 'v' and 'g') cannot be easily represented in the standard Arabic script. Similarly, in the next example, when (re)contextualised into the Arabic script, the English name 'Big Value SUPERMARKET' becomes 'biij faaliu subrmaarkt'. Clearly, several transformations can be found. These are again to do with the inherent differences/incompatibility between the two writing systems. That is, the existing Arabic script cannot readily represent certain sounds in English. As a result, sounds such as 'g' (as in 'big'), 'v' (as in 'value') and 'p' (as in 'supermarket') are respectively rendered as 'j', 'f' and 'b'. In many of these examples, the transliterated versions in Arabic have undergone significant changes so much so that they are all but unrecognisable (if not placed alongside the respective English versions).

Figure 6 features more examples of English being 'spelled' using the Arabic script. These include single words (e.g. 'feel'), phrases ('the healthier option', 'the healthy home', 'yes to less') and idiomatic expressions in English (e.g. 'UP AND RUNNING'). Notably, the Arabic name for 'UP AND RUNNING' is transliterated as 'ab and raniingh' in the Arabic script. Again, as discussed elsewhere, given the limitations of the Arabic script, sounds such as 'p' and 'g' in English cannot be precisely represented using existing equivalents in the Arabic script. As such, close approximates 'b' and 'gh' are respectively used. Also, interestingly, in the 'feel' example (photographed on a paper tissue box), the English word is rendered as فيل (fiil). This,

Figure 6 Signs in Dubai

however, can be problematic and confusing as فيل means 'elephant' in standard Arabic.

More examples of this strategy can be found in Figure 7. The existence of these signs gives rise to a kind of neat parallelism, where the English information often tends to be placed on the left-hand side and the Arabic information (phonetically transliterated from English) is placed on the right-hand side. Unlike other examples where the English sound 'v' is commonly represented as 'f' in Arabic (cf. Figures 4 and 5), the 'v' sounds in the 'SEVEN' and 'LET'S VAPE' examples are respectively (re)contextualised into Arabic using ڤ. This letter traditionally is not found in the original Arabic script. Instead, this is a letter later developed to represent the 'v' sound in some other adapted scripts to write other languages. The letter ڤ is also sometimes found in certain North African Arabic dialects (e.g. Moroccan Arabic).

More examples of this phenomenon can be found in Figure 8, Figure 9, Figure 10 and Figure 11 (where the Arabic versions are transliterated phonetically from their English counterparts in a wholesale manner). In many cases, the Arabic texts are also multimodally designed to match the English versions (e.g. colour and style). BLACK & BLUE and FOOTLOOOONG COOKIE in Figure 9 are examples of this. These examples are highly telling, pointing to the fact that English has infiltrated into and become glocalised (Gorter 2006; Sharifian 2010) and disguised in the local language/script. The Arabic transliterated from English may be understood as a new and emerging type of language variety that is Arabised English or

Figure 7 Signs in Dubai

Figure 8 Signs in Dubai

Figure 9 Signs in Dubai

Multiscriptal English and Transliteration 29

Figure 10 Signs in Dubai

Figure 11 Signs in Dubai

pseudo Arabic disguised in the Arabic script. The increasingly visible presence of this linguistic phenomenon also demonstrates how English and Arabic, traditionally believed to be categorically different and distant languages that feature disparate grammatical structures and mirror different religious values and sociocultural worldviews, may co-exist and give rise to hybridity in the multilingual and super-diverse UAE. Notably, in many cases, transliterated Arabic might make no sense to Arabic native speakers with no/limited knowledge of English (Gu and Almanna 2023). Sometimes, the information in Arabic might need to be read alongside the English information to be understood. From this perspective, the transliterated Arabic (from English) may be viewed as more symbolic in nature. Please see Al Agha (2006), Gu and Almanna (2023) and Piller (2018) for more discussions about this increasingly visible phenomenon of transliterated Arabic (from English) in the MENA (Middle East and North Africa) region documented in recent years.

Having discussed English disguised in the Arabic script in a more wholesale manner in the form of certain units (e.g. words and expressions), I would like to highlight that multiscriptal English in the new script (e.g. Arabic script) can also appear alongside other authentic elements in the language, thus leading to translanguaging. For illustrative purposes, a few examples from Dubai are provided here (Figure 12). In the first example, the Arabic version for 'GRAND PARKING' is 'مواقف الجراند' (mwaqf aljrand). Clearly, the English word 'grand' morphs into Arabic and appears as 'jrand'. As discussed elsewhere, no sound in the Arabic alphabet can accurately represent the sound 'g' as in 'grand' or 'great'. As such, the Arabic letter ج (j) is used as a close approximate instead. What is interesting is that ال (al) is added. In Arabic, 'al' is similar to 'the' in English. Therefore, grammatical elements have been added to the word transliterated from English. In the second example, the street name in English is 'Kite Beach St'. Yet, interestingly, the Arabic version features the authentic Arabic word for 'street' شارع and transliterated elements directly imported from English كايت بيتش (kait biitsh), thereby leading to a kind of mixing and hybridity. Notably, in the Arabic script, no letter corresponds to the 'ch' sound (as in 'beach' or 'China') in English. As such, in the transliterated version, تش (tsh) is used to represent the 'ch' sound as a coping strategy. In the third example, on the label of a bottled water, the information 'Discover more cool things' and its Arabic version are visible. In the Arabic version, the message says 'إكتشف أشياء كوول' (literally 'discover things cool'. Interestingly, rather than using authentic words in Arabic for 'exciting' or 'interesting', 'كوول' (kool) is used, which is phonetically rendered from the English word 'cool'. In the next example, the English name of the medical service provider is 'ROYAL PALACE MEDICAL CENTRE'. In the Arabic version, while the overall structure of the name remains Arabic, two out of the four words in the Arabic

Figure 12 Signs in Dubai

version are transliterated phonetically from English. These are رويال (ruyaal) taken from 'royal' and بالاس (balas) taken from the word 'palace'. Again, the 'p' sound in 'palace' is represented as 'b' (ب) using the Arabic script due to a lack of readily available letter in the Arabic script. The name itself can be seen as a kind of translanguaging. In a similar vein, in the next few examples, the English words 'crispy', 'KidsFirst', 'fresh' and 'VERY SIMPLE' have been transliterated into Arabic respectively. Notably, when the English word 'fresh' is transliterated into Arabic, the grammatical element ال (al) is added, similar to the 'GRAND PARKING' example. This signifies some kind of indigenisation. These examples show that multiscriptal English in the host script can appear alongside and become indigenised in the host script/language. However, these are relatively small in number compared with the more wholesale transliteration of English into Arabic.

The trend is also widely seen in Abu Dhabi. While it is impossible to quantify the strategy's prevalence in the two cities, it seems like it is slightly less visible in Abu Dhabi than Dubai. This may be because Abu Dhabi as the capital city is the political centre and is less commercialised and touristy. A few signs are illustrated here (cf. Figure 13). In the first sign, Royal Rose is a luxurious five-star hotel in Abu Dhabi. The Arabic name 'رويال روز' [ruyal ruz] is a direct transliteration of 'Royal Rose' (notably, in the Arabic sign, certain letters are elongated/stretched for stylistic and aesthetic reasons – a phenomenon called 'kashida'). This transliteration strategy is used despite the existence of authentic Arabic words for the name. While the reason behind the strategy is unknown, transliterating from English in this case seemingly gives the hotel a luxurious and 'Western' feel. This is in line with the façade of the hotel, featuring a neoclassical style. Similarly, for the 'OUTLET STORE' and 'DAY TO DAY' examples, the respective Arabic versions also represent transliterations from the English versions. Notably, in the DAY TO DAY example, even the preposition 'to' in English is transplanted into Arabic. In the last example, the name of the travel company is 'FAST TRACK'. This is also evident in the Arabic name, which becomes 'فاست تراك' [faast traak]. This English-derived business name in the Arabic script in turn also appears in the company's logo, which is designed

Figure 13 English transliterated into Arabic in Abu Dhabi's LL

in a stylish and sophisticated way similar to the classic logo for Qatar's Al Jazeera TV station. This calligraphy style is often believed to be Islamic, giving a traditional and religious feel. However, this is just English disguised in the Arabic script. This logo itself represents a hybrid, where the Western/global and the Islamic/traditional merge into one. The (re)contextualisation of English in the Arabic name and also in the Arabic calligraphic style leads to hybridity and new identities.

Likewise, in Figure 14, the first sign (top) is a large and highly visible billboard attached to a building in Abu Dhabi. The sign is highly informative and multimodal in nature, which is about the provision of car services to customers. The most visible text in English says 'SERVICE MY CAR'. Interestingly, the 'Arabic' version 'سيرفيس ماي كار' [siirfiis maii kaar] is not authentic Arabic but an inter-scriptal rendition of English into the Arabic script. In Arabic, the 'v' sound does not exist. As such, in the Arabic version, the 'v' sound as in 'service' is realised as 'f'. This shows that when (re)contextualising English into another script (e.g. Arabic), adaptations are often needed based on what is possible in the language/script. Clearly, in the billboard, in both the English and Arabic versions, images of a car are inserted into the texts. The two

Figure 14 English transliterated into Arabic in Abu Dhabi's LL

versions are designed in a coordinated and neat way, pointing to a great degree of 'choreography' (Lee 2022). The transliterated use of Arabic is also visible in the other sign (bottom) in Figure 14, found on the wall of a supermarket called 'FILIPINO HOUSE SUPERMARKET' in Abu Dhabi.

Food items in Arabic are also often transliterated from English. The sign on the left (Figure 15) is a monolingual advertising sign in Arabic from KFC. The new item on offer for a limited time only is 'ريد هوت تويستر' [reed hoot tweestr]. This is transliterated from the English name 'Red Hot Twister'. For people with knowledge of English (and aided by the other multimodal elements in the sign), it might make sense and ring a bell. However, it may be less so for those who are not already familiar with English. For the sign on the right-hand side, it shows a bilingual menu from a fast-food restaurant called Hardee's. In a similar vein, the respective 'Arabic' names for the food item and a meal are phonetic and inter-scriptal transliterations from their corresponding English versions 'CORDON BLEU CHICKEN BITES' and 'STAR FAMILY MEAL'. Given the fact that minimal/zero additional meaning can be conveyed by the 'Arabic' versions, these Arabic versions may be seen as more symbolic or decorative (Gu and Almanna 2023) in nature.

Figure 15 Fast-food advertisements featuring transliterated Arabic from English in Abu Dhabi

As a general observation, this trend of transliterating English into the Arabic script is highly prominent in the commercialised, materialistic and glamorous Dubai and also relatively visible in Abu Dhabi. In contrast, this phenomenon is less visible in other less commercial, touristic and 'global' emirates such as Fujairah and Ras Al Khaimah. In other words, in those more remote and 'far-flung' emirates which are less influenced by tourism, globalisation and a neoliberal ideology, authentic, pure and meaningful Arabic is more widely seen. Despite a lack of systematic comparison and concrete statistical information, this shows that this linguistic practice is at least partially motivated and driven by globalisation, (foreign) capitals and neoliberalism.

7.1.2 Qatar

Having presented linguistic evidence from Dubai and Abu Dhabi in the UAE, some very brief discussions are also provided here about Qatar. As a neighbouring nation in the gulf region, Qatar shares a similar history with the UAE as a former British protectorate. Like the UAE, Qatar also features similar demographic and sociolinguistic profiles, with Arabic-speaking Qatari locals significantly outnumbered (Ahmad and Hillman 2021; Gu and Almanna 2023) by temporary foreign workers from India, Pakistan, Nepal, Bangladesh, Sri Lanka, Indonesia, the Philippines and so on.

The inter-scriptal transliteration strategy is also rather pervasive, for example, in Doha, the capital city of Qatar. This trend concerning the more symbolic and decorative transliterated use of Arabic (from English) is visible in the historical Souq Waqif area and other neighbouring parts of the old town as well as in the newly developed and super-modern areas in Doha. Figure 16 contains a few examples of this. For example, 'باندا فود سنتر' [banda fud sntr] is transliterated from 'PANDA FOOD CENTRE'. Similarly, 'سكند كب' [sknd kb] is not authentic and real Arabic but is phonetically rendered from 'SECOND CUP'.

Mirroring the observations made about Dubai and Abu Dhabi, given the wide linguistic differences between Arabic and English, some adaptations need to be made when rendering and (re)contextualising English into Arabic. This is because certain sounds cannot be expressed by the current Arabic script. In standard Arabic and most dialects, the 'p' sound does not exist. In the 'PANDA FOOD CENTRE' and 'SECOND CUP' cases, the bilabial 'p' in English is rendered into Arabic as 'ب' [b] as a coping strategy/make-shift. This helps arrive at a rough phonetic representation of English.

Potentially, adding to the complexity, and more importantly confusion, is the fact that there is rarely any fixed way of rendering English into Arabic. This often is done in a discretionary and random manner, which may exhibit the sign-author's individual style and personalised understanding of English

Figure 16 English transliterated into Arabic in Doha's LL

pronunciation. A good case in point is the transliteration of the definite article 'the' from English into Arabic phonetically. In English, 'the' can be pronounced differently, for example, as /ðiː/ or /ðə/. As such, it is not uncommon to see that the word 'the' is phonetically rendered differently in different signs, depending on different people's individual interpretations and personal styles. In the 'the gate mall' example in Figure 16, 'the' is rendered into Arabic as ذي [dhi]. Interestingly, in the 'the rice and the noodle' example, 'the' is localised and realised in Arabic as 'اذ' [dha]. Such inconsistent and even idiosyncratic ways of transliterating can add further challenges to understanding, especially for those Arabic speakers with no knowledge of English. As such, if the omnipresent visibility/presence of such language use has given rise to a new kind or variety of 'Arabic', we can clearly see that variations do exist.

As with the scenarios discussed in Dubai and Abu Dhabi, the information in 'Arabic' and English is often neatly presented, coordinated and thus highly choreographed (Lee 2022) in nature in Qatar. While this cannot be generalised to all cases, the 'Arabic' information frequently appears on the right-hand side and the English information routinely appears on the left-hand side. The (multimodal) texts in 'Arabic' and English are often well designed and formatted in terms of colour and style, where the 'Arabic' versions are usually styled in ways that match the English versions. Since English is written from left to right and Arabic is written from right to left, such arrangement seemingly creates a kind of symmetry. Figure 17 below offers some rough idea about the common stylistic design/arrangement of business signs in Qatar and other places' LL in the Gulf region.

To sum up, the linguistic landscapes in the Gulf region and the Middle East in general tend to increasingly feature 'transliterated' Arabic from English in a seemingly mechanical, symbolic, decorative and wholesale manner. Rather than two pure forms, the Arabic versions are often subordinate to the English versions. This arguably gives rise to a new genre or variety of nonsensical 'Arabic' that may not ordinarily be understood by native speakers of the language (especially for those without knowledge of English). Sometimes, the 'Arabic' versions only make sense when placed alongside their corresponding English versions. Clearly, in most examples, resorting to transliteration as the 'go-to' strategy is not to do with 'untranslatability' or a lack of equivalents. Instead, this is more of a conscious and strategic decision, a stylistic preference and an ideological choice. This shows the far-reaching impact of the all-powerful English on the broader region's LL and linguistic ecology in an unprecedented way against a backdrop of globalisation, neoliberalism, increasing (super)diversity and frequent language contact. Of these, business and market forces (Edelman and Gorter 2010) notably may constitute an important factor in the linguistic landscape of the more developed and commercialised gulf region. In many ways, in a context of globalisation and neoliberalism, the business owners are arguably 'interpellated' (Althusser 2014) ideologically as subjects, believing that such language use (e.g. transliterating from English) is cool, trendy and 'international'. Globalisation and neoliberalism, as major and powerful ideologies in the twenty-first century, arguably constitute 'the routine material logic of everyday life' (Eagleton 2007: 37) and possess the power to shape language use by social actors. The linguistic practice of

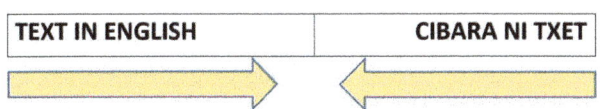

Figure 17 A common symmetrical design of signage with English (written from left to right) and transliterated 'Arabic' (written from right to left).

transliteration can be viewed as a concrete textual and discursive manifestation of such market-driven ideologies on the place's LL in a globalised world. In contrast, this strategy/linguistic practice of inter-scriptal transliteration (from English) is seemingly less visible in North Africa. Presumably, this is partly because the Gulf region has been more influenced by the British Empire and more recently the trend of globalisation and consumerism. In comparison, Arabic-speaking countries and regions in (North) Africa (e.g. Morocco, Tunisia, Algeria, Mauritania and Chad) have been historically influenced by France and the French language and have been less 'international' and commercialised than global cities such as Dubai and Qatar in the gulf.

7.2 Brunei, Malaysia and the Malay World

Malay (also Indonesian, a variety of Malay) is the official/national language in much of the Malay world (e.g. Malaysia, Indonesia, Brunei and Singapore). The Roman script (or Rumi) is widely used in writing the language in the Malay world now, partly as a result of its contact with the Europeans and the broader trend of globalisation. The Jawi writing system (cf. Coluzzi 2022), as an adapted and modified version of the Arabic script, was traditionally dominant in writing Malay as part of the Islamisation process of the region. The use of Jawi to write Malay indexes a strong sense of religious and cultural identity. However, Jawi increasingly represents an endangered orthography in many parts of the Malay world (Coluzzi 2022). That is, while Jawi is still very much alive and well in Brunei, it is now only visible in parts of Malaysia, Indonesia and some areas in Southern Thailand (e.g. Pattani) as a result of the decline. If the employment of Rumi (the Roman script) indexes a modern and global identity, Jawi is more connected with the region's Islamic heritage and cultural traditions.

The dynamic interactions between English and Malay in the Roman script (e.g. some kinds of translanguaging) are not uncommon and this is already well documented. What is particularly salient and interesting is the relationship between Malay in Jawi and English. In this section, I demonstrate how English and its multifarious manifestations have even made inroads into Malay written in the Arabic-based Jawi script in places which may be perceived as being very traditional, conservative and religious to outsiders. To this end, linguistic landscape data from Brunei and parts of Malaysia (e.g. Kelantan and Terengganu) are presented and discussed.

7.2.1 Brunei

Let us first turn our attention to Brunei, a country that is part of the Malay-speaking world. Situated on the northern coast of Borneo, Brunei is a small and rich country in Southeast Asia. As with other countries in the broader region, Brunei has traditionally been shaped by various cultures, languages and religions over centuries. Islam notably took root and became established in Brunei since around the fourteenth century. In its more recent history, Brunei became a British protectorate in 1888 and was heavily influenced by the British Empire in various aspects before it became independent in 1984. As a result of the country's history, Malay is the country's official language and English is also widely used. The vital role of English in the country and more specifically Brunei English has been explored in great detail in Deterding and Sharbawi (2013). While Malay is closely linked to Malayness and an Islamic identity, English represents the international and global side of the country (Coluzzi 2016; Deterding and Sharbawi 2013). The Arabic-adapted Jawi script (written from right to left) is one of the two official scripts in Brunei. Figure 18 shows

Figure 18 English transliterated into Jawi in Brunei's LL

how English is (re)contextualised and internalised in the Arabic-derived Jawi script in Brunei's bottom-up signs (signage from businesses of varying sizes) in the country's LL through transliteration.

Similar to the scenarios in the UAE and Qatar, in those signs, the information in Malay (Jawi script) is written from right to left and tends to be mostly placed on the right-hand side or placed at the top. Also, generally speaking, given the neat presentation, most signs may be understood as highly choreographed (Lee 2022) in nature, with the English and Malay information being more or less equally prominent. Such an arrangement is neat and well coordinated, giving a sense of equilibrium and equitability. It might be common expectation that the two seemingly equal versions are two pure forms in the respective languages. However, the Malay versions in Jawi are but transliterations from the information-rich English versions. As indicated in Figure 18, these, for instance, include RUN TRAIL NATION (Malay version: rn triil niishn). In the last two signs, the Malay versions are wholesale transliterations from the sentences in English 'IT'S A GRIND COFFEE HOUSE' and 'IT'S A GREAT COFFEE HOUSE', respectively. Notably, for example, in the 'IT'S A GREAT COFFEE HOUSE' example, the Malay version reads like [iiit's "a griit kofii ha"us]. Such inter-scriptal rendition at a sentential level reminds us of the Pandora example discussed earlier (Figure 1 found in Dubai's LL). Such whole-sale rendition at a sentential level is fascinating, given often the unmarked and relatively simple and straightforward nature of the sentences (where transliteration is not necessary). For instance, 'IT'S A GREAT COFFEE HOUSE' can be easily conveyed semantically as 'ini kedai kopi yang bagus/keren/mantop/hebat' in Malay/Indonesian to render the actual meaning. Clearly, this is not a purely linguistic decision but a stylistic and ideological choice, which prefers and idolises English. This betrays an underlying ideological belief that rendering English phonetically into the local script/language is 'cool' and fashionable. Interestingly, even the apostrophe ', ' has been added to the Malay versions, thus creating similar visual and aesthetic effects that match the corresponding apostrophes in the English versions. This shows how the local language/script often plays second fiddle to the powerful English.

Also, as observed in the transliteration practices in the Gulf context, there is usually no fixed and universally accepted way of transliterating. For example, for the indefinite article 'A', it is realised differently in the last two signs in Figure 18 (circled in red). Clearly, just as the English article 'a' may be pronounced differently by different people in different contexts (e.g. for emphasis purposes), the transliteration may also vary, depending on different individuals' interpretations of the sound. This points to flexibility, individual style and even idiosyncrasy in transplanting and glocalising English into local languages multiscriptally.

As discussed earlier, a few sounds (e.g. 'g' and 'p') cannot be adequately represented using existing Arabic script (cf. discussions about the UAE and Qatar's LLs earlier). In the Arabic-derived Jawi script, notably a few letters have been invented based on the original Arabic script. These invented letters include ڤ [p], چ [ch], and ڬ [g]. The ڬ [g] sound, for example, involves an additional dot added to the Arabic letter for 'k'. To some extent, the improved Jawi script (designed for writing Malay) also turns out to be better equipped for transliterating other languages (e.g. English) into the script. For instance, the 'g' sound as in English words such as 'grind' and 'great' in Figure 18 (which otherwise would have been rendered into the Arabic script using other 'close' alternatives such as a 'j' or 'q' sound) now can be directly rendered into the Jawi script using the letter ڬ [g].

More examples of this transliterated use of language can be found in Figures 19, 20 and 21, where the Malay (Jawi) versions are directly transliterated from their

Figure 19 English transliterated into Jawi in Brunei's LL

Figure 20 English transliterated into Jawi in Brunei's LL

Figure 21 English transliterated into Jawi in Brunei's LL

English counterparts. As briefly alluded to earlier, the 'improved' Jawi script with the invention of letters such as ڤ [p], چ [ch], and ݢ [g] is better positioned to 'spell' English (compared with the original Arabic script). In other words, the various sounds in English can be more accurately expressed using the 'improved' script, thus leading to better correspondence. For example, compared with the original Arabic script, the 'g' sound as in 'BURGER KING' (Figure 19) and 'Good Home' (Figure 21) as well as the 'p' sound as in 'the body shop' (Figure 20) and 'focus point' (Figure 21) can be more directly represented in the improved Jawi script, using ݢ and ڤ respectively.

Again, the inter-scriptal transliteration from English using the local script may not always make sense as far as the conveyance of semantic meaning is concerned. Similar to our discussions on the gulf region (e.g. the UAE and Qatar), many instances of such language use are not to do with a lack of equivalents or an inability for the local language Malay to convey similar meanings. For instance, 'makan tengah hari dengan lada' would mean 'Pepper Lunch' (Figure 19). Similarly, for the rather plain-sounding business name 'GOOD HOME', an obvious literal version in Malay would be 'rumah yang bagus/baik' (Figure 21). From a marketing perspective, rendering English into local language/script may give an exotic flavour and make the business name/brand sound 'cool' and international. Yet, this arguably is done at the expense of more effective communication of the actual meaning to some locals. The pervasive nature of such language use gives rise to a new type of English glocalised and disguised in the local script, adding to the locale's linguistic ecology.

7.2.2 Malaysia (Kelantan and Terengganu)

Having explored the phenomenon in Brunei (where Jawi is pervasive as an official script in the country), let us now focus on the Malaysian context. In Malaysia in general, Jawi is less used and is, for Coluzzi (2022), even endangered. For example, in the global metropolis Kuala Lumpur and some other parts of Malaysia, the use of the Arabic-based Jawi script can range from being not very visible to even minimal. In these places, apart from religious venues, Jawi can more or less be found in and around government organisations, departments and venues relating to culture, religion, heritage and so on. Figure 22 contains three out of not many examples where English is transliterated fully or partially into the Arabic-derived script in Kuala Lumpur. In the photo (on top), the sign is found in a halal restaurant in central Kuala Lumpur close to the iconic Petronas Twin Towers. 'باربيكيو نايتس' [barbiikiiu naaiits] is a transliteration from 'BBQ NIGHTS'. Since Kuala Lumpur is a city in a

Figure 22 English fully or partially transliterated into Jawi in Kuala Lumpur's LL

Malay-speaking country, we have reasons to believe that this is Malay written in the Jawi script. However, since the area near KLCC (Kuala Lumpur City Centre) is popular among businessmen and tourists from the Middle East, this can also be understood as 'Arabic'. Similarly, the restaurant owner and staff are Pakistani. This can also be thought of as Urdu, which also uses an Arabic-based script. The strategic use of transliteration here may simultaneously serve some basic communication purposes to people from different linguistic and cultural backgrounds, given that the Arabic script is shared by different languages (e.g. Arabic, Malay in Jawi, Urdu, Pakistani Punjabi, Sindhi, Farsi). The multilingual sign (middle) in Figure 22 is from a local Malaysian restaurant found in the Suria KLCC mall, which specialises in Penang food. The content in Malay (Jawi script) is 'كداي كوفي لتتل ڤينڠ' [kedai kopi lttl pinang]. Clearly, elements from English (e.g. 'little' as in 'little penang') have been partly transliterated and inserted into the Malay structure. Notably, the Malay name in the Jawi script features different grammatical structure and word order from English (where the nature of the business 'kedai kopi' or a kafe is frontloaded at the beginning of the name). In comparison, the Chinese name 小檳城美食館 is pure Chinese, which is a rendition of the name semantically. In the last sign (Figure 22 bottom), it is an advertising sign about Kelantan as a tourist destination found in Kuala Lumpur's international airport. Clearly, English (LET'S EXPLORE KELANTAN), Malay in the Latin script (JOM TEROKAI) and Malay in Jawi can be found in the sign. What is fascinating is that the 'Malay' information written in the Arabic-derived Jawi script (liit's iiiksploor Kelantan) is not based on the Malay version in Latin script but is transliterated from the English version 'LET'S EXPLORE KELANTAN' (even the apostrophe is replicated). This points to a fascinating case of multiscriptal English.

While not widely seen in places like Kuala Lumpur, Jawi is routinely used and compulsory for businesses (e.g. shop signs) in the north-eastern states of Kelantan and Terengganu in Malaysia (Coluzzi 2022) in principle. Indeed, Kelantan and Terengganu are arguably some of the more conservative and 'Islamic' places in Malaysia, featuring higher-than-average percentages of Muslim population. For illustrative purposes, LL data from Kota Bharu (Figure 23) and Kuala Terengganu (Figure 24), the respective capital cities of Kelantan and Terengganu, are presented and explored briefly. As seen in the data, English names have been (re)contextualised and localised into the Jawi script. While individual signs can vary in terms of style and design, as a general observation, in these places examined, English in the Latin script tends to be often more prominent than or as prominent as Malay (Jawi). This is seemingly slightly different from the scenarios observed in Brunei, where English and Malay (Jawi) are more or less of equal prominence.

In Figure 23 taken from Kelantan's capital Kota Bharu's LL, all the Malay texts in Jawi are phonetic transliterations from 'Origin of Great Taste', 'RedZone DotCom CENTRE', 'SBB TEXTILES', 'JEWELS HOTEL', 'HAPPY HOME', 'U & ME RESTAURANT', 'Butter & Cream' and 'Penny Fashion' respectively. It is fascinating to see both nouns and grammatical elements (e.g. 'of') in the expression/phrase 'Origin of Great Taste' are rendered into Malay as 'اوريجين اوف ڬرات تاس' [aoriijiin aof graat taas]. Again, the strategy of transliteration is not always for pure linguistic reasons as many common words do exist to help convey the same/similar ideas as English. For instance, 'Great Taste', 'RedZone', 'CENTRE' would be 'rasa hebat/enak', 'Zon Merah' and 'PUSAT' in Malay respectively. Similarly, 'rumah yang bahagia/gembira' is the literal Malay name for 'HAPPY HOME'. The decision to transliterate English sounds into Malay (Jawi) script rather than using meaningful, corresponding Malay words may be attributable to the fact that authentic local Malay names may lack snob value and are less 'cool' compared with the English-sounding ones. This illustrates the influential nature of English in our globalised world.

In Figure 24 taken from Terengganu's capital Kuala Terengganu's LL, similar trends can be found, providing further evidence concerning the inroads made by

Figure 23 English transliterated into Jawi in Kota Bharu's LL

English in the local LL. Notably, the English words 'hair saloon', 'hair studio', 'investment bank', 'MR D.I.Y.' and 'good luck' are inter-scriptally rendered into Malay (Jawi). Similarly, Syrup VS. Soda is also phonetically and inter-scriptally enacted in Jawi as 'سيرڤ وس سودا' [siirp vs suuda]. As explored in the cases taken from Brunei's LL, because the Jawi script features a few additional letters based on the Arabic script, the Jawi writing system is better positioned to transliterate sounds in English. This therefore leads to better correspondence in the inter-scriptal conversion process compared with the original Arabic script.

Multiscriptal English and Transliteration 47

Figure 24 English transliterated into Jawi in Kuala Terengganu's LL

The (re)contextualisation of English into the local language/script gives English a new manifestation, incarnation, and a new lease of life beyond just the taken-for-granted Latin script. Overall, these as well as the various multimodal elements give the urban space an interesting glocalised and hybridised identity, permitting a dynamic dialogue between the Anglo-Saxon/modern and the traditional/Islamic. The documented evidence challenges the traditional belief that the use of two languages should involve two pure forms.

7.3 Singapore

Let us now turn our attention to Singapore and explore how this inter-scriptal transliteration practice is evidenced in the Southeast Asian nation's linguistic landscape. Singapore is a young and ethnolinguistically diverse country. What are current-day Singapore and Malaysia have been influenced and shaped by various languages, cultures, religions and traditions over centuries. In its more recent history, partly due to its strategic geographical location, Singapore was founded by Sir Stamford Raffles in 1819. Singapore, as a UK colony, was an important part of the British Empire until its independence in 1965. Over time, for a myriad of historical, sociopolitical and economic reasons, the Chinese, Malays and Indians have become the three major established ethnic groups (Jain 2021; Lim 2004) in the country in addition to other ethnic minority groups. Corresponding to the ethnic make-up, Chinese, Malay and Tamil are recognised as three official languages in addition to English (Leimgruber 2013; Lim 2004; Schneider 2007).

Chinese Singaporeans make up the majority in Singapore (roughly 75 per cent of the country's population). As a result, Mandarin Chinese as well as other Chinese varieties/dialects such as Cantonese, Hokkien, Hakka, Teochew and Hainanese are spoken. In addition, given the existence of Malay-speaking Singaporeans and given the fact that the city state is surrounded by Austronesian languages in the Malay world (e.g. Malaysia, Indonesia, Brunei and Southern Thailand), Malay is an official language and also a (symbolic) national language, permitting Singapore to maintain some sort of cultural ties with its Malay/Indonesian-speaking neighbours. Also, the Dravidian language Tamil represents an official language in the city state, which is the language of the Tamils who were brought to Singapore and also current-day Malaysia from South India as indentured labourers (Jain 2021) during the colonial era. Additionally, other languages from the Indian subcontinent (e.g. Punjabi, Hindi, Gujarati, Urdu, Nepali, Bengali, Malayalam and Telugu) and various migrant languages (e.g. Tagalog) can also be heard to varying degrees as a result of migration and the movement of people from different periods (Jain 2021). Yet, these languages do not have official statuses. In Singapore's post-colonial linguistic ecology, English is the unchallenged and dominant language, lingua franca and unifying code of great instrumental value (Lee 2022; Zhang, Tupas and Norhaida 2020), which brings different ethnolinguistic groups together. The dominant position of English in Singapore is also a result of the country's deliberate bilingual language policy since independence, and a product of its modern/western orientation as a major business hub (Leimgruber 2013; Schneider 2007). Singapore's ethnolinguistic situation, English in Singapore and more specifically Singapore English are widely discussed, which can be found in Leimgruber (2013), Lim (2004), Low & Pakir (2018) and Schneider (2007).

Given the focus of this Element, Singapore's MRT stations are used as an entry point to help shed light on the importance of transliteration in the making of the city's multilingual LL. The general naming practices of Singapore's MRT stations have been discussed in Lim & Perono Cacciafoco (2023). The general multilingual ecology in Singapore has been covered in Leimgruber (2013), Lim (2004) and Lee (2022). In Singapore's MRT system, the four official languages are visible and present to varying extent in the written linguistic landscape. Notably, due to the fact that both English and Malay use the Latin script and because some English station names already feature Malay-derived names (e.g. Bukit Batok, Paya Lebar, Tanah Merah and Tanjong Pagar), the English and Malay station names are usually shared and are, thus, the same (which also saves some space). As a general observation, Chinese station names tend to be authentic and rich in meaning, which may be originally from Chinese and various Chinese dialects in the first place or may be translated into Chinese semantically. As such, what is of particular interest is Tamil station names in the MRT system. Actually, many Tamil station names tend to be transliterated directly from their English counterparts into the Tamil writing system. This is illustrated in Figure 25. The corresponding English and Tamil names are also

Figure 25 Tamil station names transliterated from English in Singapore's MRT system

provided in Table 1. Tang (2020) and Zhang, Tupas and Norhaida (2020) have recognised that in Singapore's multilingual language ecology there is a pecking order and English plays the most dominant role amongst the four official languages. This is rightly the case in many contexts in Singapore. Tamil is often at the bottom of the pecking order. That is, as far as the city state's written MRT station names are concerned, Tamil is seemingly the least powerful of the four official languages. This is not only because very few, if any, MRT station names are based on Tamil (where in contrast many station names are English, Chinese and Malay in origin). This is also in the sense that a significant number of Tamil station names are not authentic or original names but phonetic transliterations from other languages (notably English) in a wholesale manner – which may be understood as an inter-scriptal manifestation of the all-powerful English in the Tamil writing system. Saliently, rather than using an authentic and original ethnic name for the Indian and South Asian neighbourhood 'Little India', the 'Tamil' name for the area is simply லிட்டில் இந்தியா (Liṭṭil intiyā), which is

Table 1 English station names and the transliterated Tamil station names in Singapore's MRT system

Station names in English	Station names in Tamil
Marina Bay	மரீனா பே (Marīnā pē)
Outram Park	ஊட்ரம் பார்க் (Ūtram park)
Queenstown	குவீன்ஸ்டவுன் (Kuvīnstavuṉ)
Farrer Park	ஃபேரர் பார்க் (Hpērar park)
Bright Hill	பிரைட் ஹில் (Pirait hil)
Chinatown	சைனாடவுன் (Caiṉāṭavuṉ)
Holland Village	ஹாலந்து வில்லேஜ் (Hālantu villēj)
Pioneer	பயனியர் (Payaniyar)
Beauty World	பியூட்டி வோர்ல்ட் (Piyūṭṭi vōrlṭ)
Admiralty	அட்மிரல்ட்டி (Aṭmiralṭṭi)
Orchard	ஆர்ச்சர்ட் (Ārccarṭ)
Bayfront	பேஃபிராண்ட் (Pēhpiraṇṭ)
Clarke Quay	கிளார்க் கீ (Kiḷārk kī)
Sixth Avenue	சிக்ஸ்த் அவென்யூ (Cikst aveṉyū)
Stadium	ஸ்டேடியம் (Sṭēṭiyam)
King Albert Park	கிங் ஆல்பர்ட் பார்க் (Kiṅ ālparṭ pārk)
Commonwealth	காமன்வெல்த் (Kāmaṉvelt)
Little India	லிட்டில் இந்தியா (Liṭṭil intiyā)
Great World	கிரேட் வோர்ல்ட் (Kirēṭ vōrlṭ)
Raffles Place	ராஃபிள்ஸ் பிளேஸ் (Rāhpils pilēs)
Promenade	புரொமனாட் (Puromaṉāṭ)
Fort Canning	ஃபோர்ட் கெனிங் (Hpōrṭ keṉiṅ)

Figure 26 English transliterated into Tamil in Singapore's bottom-up LL

phonetically transliterated from the English name. More examples of this can be found in Table 1. Whatever the reasons might be behind this phenomenon, Tamil is seemingly at the receiving end of the powerful English in Singapore's postcolonial linguistic ecology.

Beyond Singapore's more top-down LL as evidenced in Tamil MRT station names in the country's public transportation system, at a bottom-up level (e.g. small businesses), the phenomenon is also visible. This is illustrated in Figure 26, where the English names SHRI KANDAA'S MOBILES and TAMILAN EXPRESS CARGO in Singapore's Little India area are respectively (re)contextualised and transliterated into the Tamil script. This phenomenon is not just restricted to Tamil but is very much reflective of the overall trend in the Indian subcontinent in general (e.g. India, Pakistan, Bangladesh and Nepal), where English has infiltrated into such languages as Punjabi, Nepali, Bengali, Tamil, Hindi and also notably Urdu (cf. Gu and Manan 2024; Hussain, Iqbal, and Saleem 2022; Manan et al. 2017; Mahmood et al. 2021).

7.4 Hong Kong SAR, China

Let us now turn our attention to Hong Kong. Hong Kong is a major financial centre and business hub in Asia. Initially a fishing village in Southern China, Hong Kong was taken by the British from the then-ruling Qing dynasty in a series of unequal treaties starting from around the 1840s. After around 156 years of British colonial rule, Hong Kong became a special administrative region

(SAR) of China in 1997. In post-colonial Hong Kong, the Biliteracy and Trilingualism policy is in place (Bolton 2000; 2002; Li 2017; Poon 2006). That is, in addition to written Chinese and written English, spoken Cantonese, spoken Mandarin and spoken English are also officially recognised. This linguistic policy is in line with the sociolinguistic situation that Hong Kong has an ethnic Chinese majority with Cantonese being the dominant spoken variety of Chinese and is in keeping with the fact that Mandarin and English are also of great importance to the city for various historical, practical and commercial reasons (notably the use of Mandarin is on the rise as a result of recent migration and incoming tourists from mainland China and language policy after the handover). Correspondingly, written Chinese (traditional Chinese characters) and written English are two most visible languages (Bolton 2000; 2002) on Hong Kong's linguistic landscape (Lai 2013; Song 2020). However, given the fact that Hong Kong is one of the most diverse global cities in the region, other minority languages (e.g. Hindi, Urdu, Nepali, Punjabi, Tagalog and Indonesian) are also visible in the city's LL to some extent (Gu 2023b; 2023c). The general linguistic situation in Hong Kong can be found in Li (2017) and the specific role of English in Hong Kong can be found in Bolton (2000; 2002) and Poon (2006).

While no language is completely impervious to influences from other languages, as a general observation, Chinese is relatively speaking a more pure and conservative language and features relatively limited borrowings from other languages. Historically, some of the (limited) influences include words localised in Chinese that were originally from Sanskrit and/or Indian languages partly through the spreading of Buddhism in ancient China and also the introduction of Japanese-made words using Chinese characters several decades ago (e.g. words relating to science, technology and Western society, philosophy and system). More recently, against a backdrop of globalisation, a limited number of words (mostly from English) have been introduced to Chinese (e.g. Wi-Fi and iPhone). However, unlike the cases in other languages, overall the influences of foreign languages on Chinese are rather limited in nature and Chinese is more resistant to the hegemony of English for various political and ideological reasons (e.g. to keep the Chinese language 'pure' and less influenced by Western culture). As such, many foreign names, concepts and so on tend to be largely translated into Chinese semantically, where the transfer of actual meaning is still privileged. Admittedly, this is also partly because the Chinese script is based on Chinese characters and is not phonologically motivated.

Nevertheless, English very occasionally may make its way into the language in the form of Chinese characters. Unlike other alphabet-based systems, this is done through finding Chinese characters that sound similar to certain English words. This is particularly salient in the Hong Kong SAR, partly as a result of its history as a former British colony. As a dynamic global metropolis and a predominantly Cantonese-speaking city historically influenced by English, Hong Kong in many ways represents an interesting language contact situation. Because of its unique East-meets-West status, a (small) number of English words have over time morphed into the local variety of Chinese. That is, a few indigenised/localised Cantonese words originally from English can be found (cf. Table 2 for typical examples).

For illustrative purposes, on Hong Kong's (post)colonial linguistic landscape (cf. Figure 27), English words such as 'taxi', 'number', 'brother' and 'store' have morphed into Chinese as 的士 (dik si), 冧把 (lam baa), 巴打 (ba da) and 士多 (si do) respectively. These are visible on both moveable objects (e.g. the city's iconic taxis and double-decker trams) and also fixed locations (e.g. shopfronts and restaurant signs).

Given the considerable phonological differences between English and Cantonese and also Chinese in general, the resulting words (adapted from English) tend to undergo significant shifts in pronunciation on different levels. For example, 'taxi' and 'number' become 'dik si' and 'lam baa'. Similarly, 'brother' and 'store' become indigenised as 'ba da' and 'si do' in the Cantonese variety of Chinese. Clearly, it is not uncommon to see major changes and transformations in vowels and also sometimes consonants. Since similar-sounding Chinese characters are used to match English sounds, the resulting localised words take on significant Cantonese/Chinese characteristics in the process, given the differences between the two languages.

Compared with other contexts discussed, instances of English disguised in Chinese characters are limited in number and mostly are restricted to individual words (rarely at phrasal and sentential levels). Despite the small number, these words borrowed from English have become naturalised and taken-for-granted

Table 2 Examples of English indigenized in Chinese characters

Cantonese	Rough pronunciations	Words in English
孖展	maa zin	margin
巴打	ba da	brother
巴士	baa si	bus
的士	dik si	taxi
冧把	lam baa	number
士多	si do	store
忌廉	gei lim	cream
撻	taat	tart

Figure 27 English words morphed into Cantonese/Chinese in Hong Kong's LL

as 'local' when written in Chinese. Arguably, at the beginning of the English-to-Cantonese conversion, the process was similar to phonetic transliteration. Over time, these words become established and entrenched in Cantonese after repeated use.

In addition to Chinese and English in Hong Kong, other languages are also visible in the global city's LL. Indeed, Hong Kong represents a most diverse place in the region. For historical reasons, the British brought Indians, Pakistanis and Nepalis (Gurkha soldiers) to Hong Kong during the colonial period, for example, to serve as soldiers and policemen. Notably, soldiers of South Asian backgrounds (e.g. Hindus, Muslims and Sikhs) were stationed in Whitfield Barracks (currently Kowloon Park in Tsim Sha Tsui) amongst other locations. This partially explains why the adjacent areas Tsim Sha Tsui, Jordan and Yau Ma Tei in the Yau-Tsim-Mong District now feature a concentration of South Asians, where Hindi, Punjabi, Urdu and Nepali signs are visible (cf. Gu 2023b; 2023c). In the South Asian communities, English is routinely transliterated into their respective languages/scripts.

In Figure 28, the first sign is about a halal meat shop in the Haiphong Road Temporary Market outside the Kowloon Park in Tsim Sha Tsui. Interestingly, the English name SHENG HING COLD MEAT Cold Halal Chicken Mutton & Beef is completely rendered into the Arabic-based Urdu script phonetically as 'shng hng kold meet kold halal chkn mtn aeend beef', despite the fact that common everyday words such as 'cold', 'chicken', 'mutton' and 'beef' are readily available in Urdu and are not newly introduced items/concepts from the West. The second, third and fourth signs in Urdu in Figure 28 are found in the famous Chungking Mansions. Featuring many South Asian and African restaurants, hotels and shops, the Chungking Mansions is hailed as an example of twenty-first-century low-end globalisation (Mathews 2008). Again, the texts

Figure 28 English transliterated into Urdu in Hong Kong's LL

in Urdu 'tayaji islamik bk siintr', 'chakwal intrniishnl heir siiloon' and 'Gujrat faast food siintr' are respectively transliterated from 'TAYAJI ISLAMIC BOOK CENTER', 'Chakwal international hair saloon' and 'GUJRAT FAST FOOD CENTRE'. It is unclear why 'book' is rendered as بک (bk) with the vowel not explicitly indicated, whereas in rendering 'food' into Urdu the vowel is made explicit. There is arguably always an element of randomness and arbitrariness in the initial rendering process. Over time, certain norms and conventions may emerge. In another example featuring Pakistani community's language use in the UK (cf. Figure 60), 'book' is also rendered into the Urdu script as 'bk', thus pointing towards some conventionalised or habitualised ways of inter-scriptal rendering. More detailed discussions of this can be found in Section 7.10.

Similarly, there are a few Urdu signs in Figure 29. The first three signs were found in Jordan/Yau Ma Tei. The Urdu names in these signs are respectively phonetically rendered from 'quality foods', 'Bismil BBQ Market' and 'NEW Chakwal Hair Cut Salon' in English. In the fourth sign found in Sham Shui Po, the Urdu names for common everyday food items 'mutton', 'chicken' and 'beef' are all transliterated from English. In the next sign also found in Sham Shui Po, the South Asian barbershop's name in Urdu is figured prominently. It reads 'atk heer-kt' in Urdu calligraphic style. Despite the seemingly exotic and traditional style/design, it is actually directly transliterated from 'Attock Hair Cut'. In the next sign about a store in Tsuen Wan, the Urdu text says 'bismillah groosri aiind fiishn stoor', which is rendered from English 'Bismillah Grocery and Fashion Store'. In other signs, English words/expressions 'Best Pakistani food', 'Extra Cup 1 dollar', 'Mango milkshake' and 'Dream Haircut' are rendered into the Urdu script. This clearly is not always due to lexical gaps as common everyday items/names such as 'book', 'hair', 'centre', 'chicken' and 'food' predate and/or are unrelated to British colonial rule and the trend of globalisation. These may be understood as English manifested and disguised in the Urdu script, hence examples of multiscriptal English.

The same phenomenon is also observed in such languages as Hindi and Nepali in post-colonial Hong Kong. In Figure 30, the first seven Nepali signs are all taken from Hong Kong's Jordan/Yau Ma Tei area. This area features a high concentration of South Asians in general and more specifically the Nepalese. For example, ग्लोबललिंक सर्भिस (glōbalaliṅka sarbhisa) is Nepali in the Devanagari script transliterated from GlobalLink Service and डाइनामिक ट्राभल्स एण्ड टुर्स (dā'ināmika ṭrābhalsa ēṇḍa ṭursa) is transliterated from DYNAMIC TRAVELS & TOURS. Interestingly, the last sign in Figure 30 is photographed from a Nepali restaurant in Yuen Long. In the Yuen Long district,

Figure 29 English transliterated into Urdu in Hong Kong's LL

the Nepalese and other south Asians can also be found for historical reasons. In this monolingual Nepali sign, what appears to be impenetrable and exotic (सिद्धार्थ फास्टफूड सेंटर or 'siddhaarth phaastaphood sentar') turns out to be transliterated from 'Siddhartha Fastfood Center'. Most of the transliterated texts from English in Figure 30 may also be understood as Hindi and can to some extent be read by other South Asians, as both Nepali and some other South Asian languages (e.g. Hindi and Marathi) share more or less the same Devanagari script. This tendency of transliterating English into local scripts resonates with the situation found in South Asia and various South Asian communities overseas (cf. Gu and Manan 2024 for focused discussions on South Asian languages such as Hindi, Punjabi, Urdu and Nepali).

Figure 30 English transliterated into Nepali in Hong Kong's LL

7.5 Nepal

Let us now shift our attention to the Indian subcontinent, a region that was influenced by the British Empire to varying degrees over the past few centuries. The tendency for English to be transliterated, (re)contextualised and embedded in South Asian languages/scripts is highly prominent for example in India and also notably Pakistan. In the Pakistani context, for instance, the transliteration of English into local languages (e.g. Urdu) is established as a highly visible trend in such places as Quetta (Manan et al. 2017), Khyber Pakhtunkhwa (Mahmood et al. 2021) and Peshawar (Hussain et al. 2022). Based on the author's observation, in Pakistan, many place, public service, administrative and infrastructure names in the local 'Urdu' versions are transliterated directly from English. It is common to see English lexical items such as 'international airport', 'railway station', 'taxation department', 'national park', 'satellite town', 'model town', 'medical centre', 'university', 'school', 'general store', 'road', 'block', 'bridge', 'sector' and 'colony' to be extensively rendered into

Multiscriptal English and Transliteration 59

the Urdu script in an inter-scriptal manner. Such transliterated language use is also widely visible in the linguistic landscapes relating to Pakistani communities overseas (please see Section 7.4 for Urdu-related LL in the global city Hong Kong and Section 7.10 for Urdu in the UK featuring this strategy).

This section specifically explores the situation in Nepal in the Indian subcontinent. With great cultural heterogeneity and ethnolinguistic diversity, Nepal is a multi-ethnic, multilingual, multi-cultural and multi-religious country (Gautam 2021; Pandey 2020) in South Asia. As a landlocked country, Nepal is geographically sandwiched between the Tibetan regions of China in the North and India in the South. Nepal, as a result, has been profoundly shaped and influenced by neighbouring areas and regions (e.g. China and India) linguistically, culturally, religiously and also in terms of food and art since ancient times (Gu 2024b). Nepal is a Hindu-majority country, whereas Buddhism is also followed. Historically, Nepal was never formally colonised by the British, unlike many countries in the region. Nevertheless, Nepal was still under considerable British influence over the years in various ways and arguably was a de facto semi-colony (Blaikie, Cameron, and Seddon 2001). Now, in terms of foreign relations, the bilateral ties with China and India, two major geopolitical players in the region, are important to Nepal.

(Socio)linguistically, various Indo-Aryan and Sino-Tibetan languages are spoken by different ethnic groups (e.g. Chhetri/Khas, Brahmin, Muslims, Newar, Rai, Gurung, Limbu, Magar, Tharu), given Nepal's geographical location. However, in this multilingual nation, Nepali is the official language and also a common lingua franca used for various kinds of formal, business and day-to-day inter-ethnic communication (Gu 2024b). An Indo-Aryan language, Nepali is believed to have descended from Sanskrit. Nepali also more or less shares the Devanagari script with languages such as Hindi and Marathi. While Nepali is dominant in Nepal's LL, English is also of importance as far as diplomacy, international relations, science, technology, commerce, business, trade, tourism, education and advertising are concerned (Pandey 2020; Sharma 2018).

As with many parts of the Indian subcontinent, English is routinely transliterated and (re)contextualised into the local Devanagari script used for writing Nepali. This trend is illustrated in Figure 31, which contains business signs found in Kathmandu and surrounding areas. These include थकाली किचेन एण्ड फाष्टफुड (Thakali Kitchen & Fast Food) and ग्राण्डी सिटी हस्पिटल (Grande City Hospital). Clearly, not just lexical items but also the entire syntactic structures are often replicated and glocalised into the local script phonetically. For example, the ampersand symbol (&) as in 'Thakali Kitchen & Fast Food' is realised as एण्ड (ēṇḍa). Similar to other locales explored, these signs

Figure 31 English transliterated into Nepali in Kathmandu's LL

demonstrate a kind of equilibrium and one-to-one correspondence between the 'Nepali' and English versions in terms of both the content and design. As such, they may be understood as being choreographed (Lee 2022) in nature, due to the neat presentation.

More interestingly, it is not uncommon to see English disguised in what appears to be Nepali monolingualism. That is, in certain signs, what appears to be written in pure Nepali to the outsider turns out to be English written in the Devanagari script. This saliently indexes the power of English and its deep-rooted impact on local languages in the twenty-first century. This is illustrated in Figure 32. The three signs in the figure are रेडिमेड फेसन हाउस (ready-made fashion house), मनोज फ्रेस मिट शप (Majoj Fresh Meat Shop) and सुप्रीति फेन्सी स्टोर (Supriti fancy Store). It remains to be seen whether the monolingual 'Nepali' signs featuring advanced English words such as 'ready-made' and 'fancy' can or cannot be understood by the general public. This is nonetheless fascinating, given the existence of readily available authentic words such as 'fresh', 'meat', 'shop' and 'store' in Nepali. These are arguably the most salient examples of 'multiscriptal English' theorised in this Element. The surreptitious and covert enactment/transplantation of English in the local script monolingually brings into sharp relief the prominence of English saliently.

Figure 32 English disguised in monolingual Nepali signs

Table 3 shows more examples of multiscriptal English in Kathmandu's LL. While using transliteration for untranslatable brand names, food items and neologisms (e.g. Wi-Fi, iPhone and coronavirus) is justified (cf. Gu and Almanna 2023), many examples illustrated here clearly are not to do with a lack of equivalents in the native/local languages. This is more of a stylistic and ideological choice, given the 'cool' factor associated with English.

When (re)contextualised into the local script, English takes on new local flavours. For instance, when the word 'fashion' as in 'unique fashion' is rendered into the local script फेसन (phēsana), the 'sh' sound in English becomes 's'. This is because many Nepali speakers often cannot distinguish between the 's' and 'sh' sounds (Rai 2006). Therefore, English has taken on new manifestations, having a new lease of life in our globalised and commodified world. This, however, may result in somewhat unintelligible names in local languages. Understanding the information often presumes a knowledge of English. For more focused discussions on South Asian languages such as Hindi, Punjabi, Urdu and Nepali, please see Gu and Manan (2024).

Table 3 More examples of English transliterated into Nepali in Kathmandu

Names in Nepali script	Rough pronunciation	Corresponding English versions
टिप टप समोसा	tip tap samosa	Tip top samosa
काठमाडौँ फन पार्क	Kāthamādauṁ phana pārka	Kathmandu Fun Park
टिबेट गेस्ट हाउस	Tibet Gest Hāus	Tibet Guest House
रोजमेरी किचेन एण्ड कफी	Rōjamērī kicēna ēnda kaphī	Rosemary Kitchen and Coffee Shop
सत्कार बुटिक होम	Satkār Butik Hom	Satkār Boutique Home
नमस्ते स्पा	Namaste Spā	Namaste Spa
फ्रेन्डशिप कफी हाउस	Phrēndaśipa kaphī hā'usa	Friendship Coffee House
पिपल्स क्याम्पस	Pipals Kyāmpas	People's Campus
थमेल भिल्ला हेरिटेज होटल	Thamēla bhillā hēritēja hōtala	Thamel Villa Heritage Hotel
टेकर्स होम	Trekaras Hom	Trekkers Home
होटल थमेल हाउस	Hotal Thamel Hāus	Hotel Thamel House
ट्रान्सपोर्ट हायर नेपाल	Trānsaport Hāyar Nepāl	Transport Hire Nepal
युनिक फेसन	Yunika phēsana	Unique Fashion
सुप्रीति फेन्सी स्टोर	Suprīti phēnsī stōra	Suprīti fancy Store
मल्ल ट्राभल एण्ड ट्रेक्स	Malla trābhala ēnda trēksa	Malla Travel & Treks
निउ फ्लोरिस्ट	Niyu Phlorist	New Florist
म्युजिक जाम स्पेस	Myujik Jam Spaces	Music Jam Space
द कमिक क्याफे	Da kamika kyāphē	The Comic Cafe
राम मेटल वर्क्स	Rām Metal Works	Ram Metal Works
अल्टरनेटिभ टेक्नोलोजी	Altarnetibh Teknolōjī	Alternative Technology
स्काईवाक टावर	Skaivāk Tāvar	Skywalk Tower
लिटिल एन्जल्स' स्कूल	Litil Enjals' Skūl	Little Angels' School
होटल मम्स होम	Hotal Mams Hom	Hotel Mums Home

7.6 Thailand

Having explored some of the regions that used to be British colonies or were under significant colonial influences of the British Empire, let us now examine Thailand, a nation that was never formally colonised. Thailand, strategically positioned in Southeast Asia, is a Buddhist-majority nation. The country has been tremendously shaped and influenced by neighbouring regions such as India and China since ancient times. Such influences can be seen in areas such as culture, religion, language, philosophy, traditions and food. In the nation's more recent history, unlike many countries in the region that became British (e.g. Malaysia, Singapore, India and Myanmar) or French colonies (e.g. Vietnam), Thailand officially was never a colony of Western imperial powers (Baker 2012). However, Thailand was still under the influence of Western powers to some extent. Like many countries, Thailand made efforts to develop and modernise itself through learning from Western language, technology, systems, architecture and ideas. Several European style buildings along the eastern bank of the Chao Phraya River (e.g. The Holy Rosary Church, Customs House, East Asiatic Building and The Assumption Cathedral) are examples of Western-Thai contact.

Theravada Buddhism represents the country's main religion, which is followed by a majority of Thai people (about 95 per cent). Linguistically, standard Thai is enshrined as the country's sole official language. (Standard) Thai is widely used in various areas and domains such as politics, business, commerce, public administration, education, media, journalism and law. In many aspects, Thailand appears to be a rather monolingual and homogenous country (cf. Baker 2012). However, this more monolithic picture is not entirely accurate. Despite the seeming homogeneity and the de jure monolingualism, various languages, dialects and varieties are spoken on the ground. Pattani Malay, for example, is spoken in Southern Thailand near the Thailand-Malaysia border. Other languages such as Chinese, Khmer and Lao are also spoken in Thailand (Foley 2005). Notably, many Thais have full or partial Chinese ancestry due to waves of migration of people from Southern China over several centuries. Many Thai people of Chinese ancestry can no longer speak Chinese.

Against a backdrop of globalisation, Thailand pursues a tourism-driven economy reliant on foreign visitors. Given its status as a popular tourist destination, English is extensively used in various contexts and is becoming increasingly instrumental (Baker 2012). While overall people in Thailand have relatively low proficiency in English, those working in the tourism/service industry and students tend to have some working knowledge of the language. Since Thailand was never formally colonised, the country is an expanding-circle nation (cf. Kachru 1992) in WE terms. Due to increasingly frequent people-to-people contact and the market-oriented neoliberal ideology, English will continue to play an important role in various communicative, transactional and commercial contexts.

To outsiders, Thai written in the seemingly 'inscrutable' script might be a 'pure' language relatively impervious to Western linguistic influences. However, contrary to the impression, the inroads made by English on Thai are far-reaching, if not always obvious. That is, English is visible in the LLs of places like Bangkok, Pattaya and Phuket (Huebner 2006). Also, English has left an indelible mark on Thai written in the Thai script (Huebner 2006). The Thai script is believed to have derived from the Old Khmer script and indexes a Buddhist and pan-Southeast Asian identity. Created by Ram Khamhaeng the Great, the Thai script is the abugida used to write Thai. The Thai writing system contains forty-four consonant symbols and sixteen vowel symbols that can be combined into at least thirty-two vowel forms and four tone diacritics to create characters mostly representing syllables.

It is a highly visible trend for many names written in the Thai script to be transliterated from English (Phanthaphoommee and Gu 2024). For example, the Thai names for many high-profile shopping malls are not authentic Thai but transliterations from English. For example, the respective Thai names for major shopping malls in central Bangkok (cf. Figure 33) สยามพารากอน (S̄yām phārākxn), สยามสแควร์วัน (S̄yām s̄khæwr̒ wạn), and เซ็นทรัลเวิลด์ (S̄ĕnthrạl weild̒) are transliterated from their original names Siam Paragon, SIAM SQUARE ONE, CentralwOrld in English. Notably, the 'Thai' versions are often in small font size and are pushed to the corners.

Given the distant nature of Thai and English, when English is transliterated into Thai, it adopts a Thai flavour in a way that fits the rules and preferences of the language. To give an idea of what the English word 'centralworld' (stylised as CentralwOrld) sounds like when rendered into Thai script as เซ็นทรัล เวิลด์ (s̄ĕnthrạl weild̒), we may have a listen of this audio here.[1]

Within or next to the Siam Paragon Mall, it is also common to see direction signs (cf. Figure 34) which contain Thai place and business names that are almost exclusively transliterated from their English counterparts. Obviously, this strategy focuses on the conveyance of sound at the expense of meaning. For

Figure 33 English transliterated into Thai in major shopping malls in Bangkok

---

[1] https://forvo.com/search/%E0%B9%80%E0%B8%8B%E0%B9%87%E0%B8%99%E0%B8%97%E0%B8%A3%E0%B8%B1%E0%B8%A5%E0%B9%80%E0%B8%A7%E0%B8%B4%E0%B8%A5%E0%B8%94%E0%B9%8C/.

Figure 34 Transliterated Thai in direction signs

example, the English name 'Sealife Bangkok Ocean World' is informative enough to give one the idea that this is an aquarium. However, the transliterated Thai version ซีไลฟ์ แบงคอก โอเชียน เวิร์ล (Sī lif̂ bængkhxk xo cheīyn weiřl) is hardly informative and cannot provide enough clues about the business involved. Interestingly, in the transliterated Thai version, แบง คอก (bængkhxk) is even used. In authentic Thai, Bangkok is more commonly called กรุงเทพมหานคร (Krung Thep Maha Nakhon). Also, interestingly, in Thai, the 'world' parts as in 'centrawOrld' and 'Sealife Bangkok Ocean World' are transliterated differently. Therefore, consistent with the observations made earlier, when English is glocalised in the local language/script, there is often no fixed approach. This can be highly individualistic and even idiosyncratic, depending on the transliterater's personalised understanding of the English pronunciation and the local language's orthography. Similarly, Figure 35 is an advertising billboard in front of the Intercontinental Hotel. In the sign, most business/service names in English are transliterated into the Thai script phonetically in small font size.

There are more examples of this in Figure 36. Clearly, the Thai versions have been transliterated directly from the English names 'ASIA BAKERY' (เอเชีย เบเกอรี่), The Pizza Company (เดอะ พิซซ่า คอมปะนี), FLASH COFFEE (แฟลช คอฟฟี่), Evergreen

Figure 35 Small-font Thai transliterated from English in a big billboard

Figure 36 Transliterated small-font Thai pushed to the corners

Place Siam (เอเวอร์กรีน เพลส สยาม) and truecoffee (ทรูคอฟฟี่). Again, the Thai versions tend to be in small font size and are pushed towards the corners, whereas the English versions are foregrounded and made front and centre. This seemingly gives the place a more 'Western' image, thus indexing a kind of global identity. This interestingly is achieved in a way that the local language does not unduly jeopardise or harm the positive 'international' image the country wishes to paint. To some extent, this betrays an underlying mentality in terms of how Thailand perceives its relationship *vis-à-vis* the west and the world cognitively. This arguably leads to 'small-print' bilingualism/multilingualism (cf. Gu 2023a). In these cases, the local languages are marginalised/backgrounded so that the Western/global face the place wishes to portray and highlight can be foregrounded and made prominent. This is widely observable in Bangkok (Phanthaphoommee and Gu 2024).

Figure 37 features more examples of this, where English morphs into the local script and is taken for granted as 'Thai'. In many/most of the examples, transliterating English into Thai is a conscious and strategic choice, a stylistic preference and/or an ideological stance worshipping the 'western'/'foreign', rather than due to 'untranslatability' or inherent limitations of Thai. Using English in various forms appears to be cool and marketable and carries snob value. For example, some in Thailand think that advertising and marketing in Thai makes the product sound cheap, whereas the advertisement is more memorable if English is made visible (Sutthinaraphan 2016). This is interesting, considering the fact that overall people in Thailand have relatively low proficiency in English (according to the EF English Proficiency Index, Thailand is in the 'Very Low Proficiency' category in 2023). This is interesting when we think about who the real audience is. That is, for those do not understand English in Thailand, the transliterated information (from English) makes little sense apart from indicating some exotic foreign-sounding names.

Table 4 contains more examples of this increasingly visible phenomenon in Bangkok. Generally speaking, when English is (re)contextualised into Thai, there are some changes in stress and intonation. Notably, for words that have first-syllable stress in English, the stress tends to be placed towards the end in Thai after inter-scriptal conversion. For example, English words 'PAragon', 'FAshion' and 'CENter' often become 'paraGON', 'faSHION' and 'cenTER' in Thai. The pronunciation[2] of เซ็นเตอร์, transliterated from 'center', is a good case in point. The same trend can be found, when 'fashion' is rendered into Thai[3] as แฟชั่น. The shift in stress pattern is also found in the 'centralwOlrd' example. This is aligned with

---

[2] https://forvo.com/word/%E0%B9%80%E0%B8%8B%E0%B9%87%E0%B8%99%E0%B9%80%E0%B8%95%E0%B8%AD%E0%B8%A3%E0%B9%8C/#google_vignette.

[3] https://forvo.com/search/%E0%B9%81%E0%B8%9F%E0%B8%8A%E0%B8%B1%E0%B9%88%E0%B8%99/.

Figure 37 More authentic examples of English transliterated into Thai script

the observation that when Thai speakers speak L2 English they often stress the final syllable and consequently lengthen the final vowel (Suntornsawet 2022).

Given the limited space, more in-depth discussions are not provided. It is clear that marketing and consumerism as part of the neoliberal ideology constitute a major shaping force (Edelman and Gorter 2010) here in structuring Bangkok's increasingly visible transliterated linguistic landscape (from English). It remains to be seen whether there is also a degree of self-colonisation here in the sense that social actors in the society have been increasingly resorting to the powerful and hegemonic language English for various marketing, commercial and practical purposes inevitably at the expense and to the detriment of the purity and integrity of the local/national language Thai. This is fascinating considering the fact that Thailand was never officially colonised by Western powers. The case of Thailand to some extent resembles the situation in the expanding-circle country South Korea also discussed in this Element.

Table 4 Other examples of English transliterated into Thai script

English version	Thai version (transliterated from English)	English version	Thai version (transliterated from English)
ICONSIAM	ไอคอนสยาม	River City Bangkok	ริเวอร์ ซิตี้ แบงค็อก
All Seasons Place	ออลซีซั่นส์เพลส	Havana Social	ฮาวาน่า โซเชียล
Newton Tower	นิวตัน ทาวเวอร์	Mango Tango	แมงโก้ แทงโก้
centralwOrld Square	เซ็นทรัลเวิลด์สแควร์	King Power International	คิง พาวเวอร์ อินเตอร์เนชั่นแนล
Siam Discovery	สยามดิสคัฟเวอรี่	Centerpoint Siam Square	เซ็นเตอร์พอยท์ สยามสแควร์
Siam Square one	สยามสแควร์วัน	One Siam	วันสยาม
Chef Man	เชฟแมน	Stadium one	สเตเดียมวัน
Siam Paragon	สยามพารากอน	Wansiri Apartment	วรรณศิริอพาร์ทเม้นท์
Siamscape	สยามสเคป	Big C Supercenter	บิ๊กซี ซูเปอร์เซ็นเตอร์
Four Points by Sheraton	โฟร์พอยท์บายเชอราตัน	Central Embassy	เซ็นทรัล เอ็มบาสซี
Pizza hut	พิซซ่าฮัท	The Platinum Fashion Mall	เดอะ แพลทินัม แฟชั่น มอลล์
All Together Suite	ออล ทูเก็ตเตอร์ สวีท	MBK Center	เอ็ม บี เค เซ็นเตอร์
The Market Bangkok	เดอะ มาร์เก็ต แบงค็อก	Bangkok Marriott Marquis Queen's Park	แบงค็อก แมริออท มาร์คีส์ ควีนส์ปาร์ค
Union Mall	ยูเนียน มอลล์	Tummy Yummy	ทัมมี่ ยัมมี่
Central Eastville	เซ็นทรัลอีสต์วิลล์	EmQuartier	เอ็มควอเทียร์
Bangkok City	บางกอกซิตี้	Holiday Inn	ฮอลิเดย์ อินน์

7.7 Russia

To add further credence to the phenomenon of 'multiscriptal English' under discussion here, in this section, I embark on an exploration of English transliterated and disguised in the Cyrillic alphabet in Russia, a country that is considered to belong to the expanding circle as far as world Englishes (WE) is concerned. The presence of English in Russia is increasingly documented in recent years. Proshina and Eddy (2016) and Ustinova (2005) have discussed the contact of English and Russian in general from different perspectives with a specific focus on Russian English. The increasingly visible presence of English in Russian cities' linguistic landscapes has also been explored by a few scholars in recent years (Aristova 2016; Bylieva and Lobatyuk 2021; Pitina 2020). Largely focusing on cities in the European part of Russia, these LL studies on the Russian context tend to be relatively brief and only discuss transliteration in passing. As such, in this section, more concrete real-world examples are provided here on the LL of Vladivostok, a city in the more remote 'far-flung' region of Russia in the Far East.

Far removed from Russia's European 'core', the port city Vladivostok is located near the border between Russia, China and North Korea in the Far East. Where Vladivostok is currently located used to be Chinese territory. However, during China's then-ruling Qing dynasty, the place was incorporated into Russian territory. At various points afterwards, there were instances of deportations and forced migrations of ethnic Chinese and notably Koreans traditionally living in the broader region to Central Asia (e.g. to Kazakhstan and Uzbekistan). Parallel to this, Vladivostok and the broader region underwent a process of Russification over time. Clearly, Russian is the dominant language in Vladivostok at present. However, to some extent, ethnic Chinese and Korean people can still be found. Given the locale's geographical location and history, the city is influenced by China and North Korea, culturally, ethnically and linguistically, to some extent. More recently, English is increasingly visible in the city, due to globalisation. The city's unique situation makes it interesting to explore in terms of how English manifests in the city's Russian-dominated LL. English in Vladivostok's LL can be overt and covert. The explicit and overt presence of English involves, for example, signage written in the Latin script monolingually or alongside Russian. In terms of the covert presence of English, traces of English are often found disguised in the local Cyrillic alphabet in Vladivostok's LL. In other words, what might be assumed as Russian by outsiders turns out to be English in disguise. The visible presence of English in Russia's LL is to do with the trend of globalisation (Ustinova 2005), where English is considered modern, cool, prestigious and marketable (Aristova 2016; Bylieva and Lobatyuk 2021; Piller 2003).

The Latin and Cyrillic alphabets are somewhat related as both writing systems stemmed from the Greek alphabet. Often, it is not uncommon to see one-to-one correspondence between certain letters. Given the limited space, a few examples taken from Vladivostok's LL are presented. In Figure 38, Шерлок Гномс (sherlok gnoms) is transliterated from 'Sherlock Gnomes', a Western-made comedy film based on the character Sherlock Holmes. In the second sign, it is a shop specialising in wine. The Russian name is ВинЛаб (vinlab), which has creatively rendered 'winelab' into Russian. In Vladivostok and Russia in general, it is also common for Western concepts such as 'supermarket' to be directly rendered into Russian phonetically as супермаркет (supermarket). The third sign is an example of this, exhibiting one-to-one Cyrillic-Latin correspondence. The place is called 'ок! Супермаркет (OK! Supermarket), which dynamically incorporates popular cultural elements from the Anglo-American culture and (re)contextualises it into the local Cyrillic alphabet. This represents a Russification of the Anglo-American. At the same time, the Russian LL becomes simultaneously anglicised. The same phenomenon is visible in other signs in Figure 38. Форвард (forvard), Калина Молл (kalina moll) and Бургер Кинг (burger king) are respectively transliterated from 'forward', 'kalina mall' and 'burger king'. These are examples of multiscriptal English written in the Cyrillic script as evidenced in a more peripheral Russian city's twenty-first-century LL. Given the shared origin of

Figure 38 English transliterated into Cyrillic alphabet in the Russian city Vladivostok

the Latin and Cyrillic writing systems, rough one-to-one correspondence can often be established. As highlighted above, when Burger King is transliterated into Russian, it becomes 'Бургер Кинг' (burger king), which is almost exactly the same as the English version. As such, as far as writing multiscriptal English in the Cyrillic script is concerned, it is seemingly a more straightforward process, compared with writing English in other distant and unrelated languages/writing systems (e.g. Arabic, Urdu, Korean and Thai).

More examples can be found in Figure 39. The first sign illustrates a souvenir shop. In the main text in Russian, the shop's name is written as Владгифтс (vladgifts). This is a transliteration from the creative English name 'vladgifts' or 'gift from Vladivostok'. The next sign is from a local hotel called СИТИ ПАРК (siti park), which is transliterated from 'city park'. The business chose this transliterated version as its Russian name presumably because of the perceived prestige and 'cool' factor related to English (cf. Aristova 2016; Bylieva and Lobatyuk 2021). The next sign is from a shop specialising in sportswear and equipment. The Russian name is Спортмастер, transliterated from 'sportmaster' in English. The rest of the signs in Figure 39 are минимаркет (minimarket), аларм сервис (alarm service), билайн (beeline), Мистер Ойл (mister oil) respectively.

The increasingly visible glocalisation of English into the local script gives rise to new identities, adding to the place's linguistic ecology. That is, elements of the Anglo-American have been added to the local LL with a Slavic base. Атлантикс Констракшн (Atlantics Construction), Интерфейс (interface), фитнес клуб (fitness club), Бэби клуб (baby club), Корал Тревел (coral travel), Тесла

Figure 39 English transliterated into Cyrillic alphabet in Russian city Vladivostok

Тревел (Tesla Travel), Сити Тур (city tour), Бизнес центр (business centre), Море-сервис (More-service) and Технопоинт (Techno Point) are some more examples of this trend. Clearly, English tends to be (re)contextualised in Vladivostok's LL particularly in businesses relating to cafes, hotels, tourism, supermarkets, high-end shopping as well as sport and fitness-related businesses and high-tech businesses, and so on. Please see Pitina (2020) for more discussions on English partially and completely appearing in other major Russian cities' linguistic landscapes. As recognised earlier, given the shared root of the Latin and the Cyrillic alphabets, rough one-to-one correspondence often exists. For example, Тесла Тревел (tesla trevel) and фитнес клуб (fitnes klub) highly resemble their English counterparts 'Tesla Travel' and 'Fitness Club'. As such, transliterating English into Russian is a relatively straightforward process. This is unlike the situations in Arabic, Urdu and also Korean, Japanese and so on, where various changes need to be made (e.g. inserting vowels and using close approximations). To some extent, given the shared European culture and tradition, this strategy also arguably has a higher degree of acceptability (the Russian language itself has been influenced by Western languages such as French historically). The documented evidence in Russia represents a telling testament to the idea of 'multiscriptal English'. This highlights the many 'faces' of English in different contexts in the twenty-first century, against a backdrop of globalisation, neoliberal ideology and consumerism.

7.8 South Korea and Korean-related Businesses Overseas

For further documented evidence on 'multiscriptal English', let us now turn to another expanding circle country, South Korea, and show how English has infiltrated into Korean in the country's linguistic landscape. Historically, the broader area of Korea (including current-day North Korea and South Korea) has been profoundly influenced and shaped by China and its language, culture and society, turning Korea into a Confucian society (Deuchler 1992) that is part of the Sinosphere. For centuries, Korean was mostly used as a spoken language and classical Chinese was the dominant code used for written communication (e.g. letters, poems, calligraphy, official documents and other written records). In other words, classical Chinese had been dominant in Korea's (written) linguistic landscape. Notably, for centuries, largely well-educated elite Koreans were able to read and write Chinese, whereas the majority of the population remained illiterate.

In view of the fundamental linguistic differences between Korean and Chinese and to promote literacy amongst the general public, a writing system used for writing Korean was invented during the period of Sejong the Great (세종대왕 or 世宗大王) in the fifteenth century to complement or as an alternative to Chinese characters. Notably, in the important historical document called Hunminjeongeum (훈민정음, 訓民正音 or literally 'the correct/proper sounds for the instruction of the people'), the rationale and logic behind devising a new writing system for the Korean language were detailed. This represents a major historical milestone in the development of the Korean language, directly paving the way for the Korean alphabet or Hangul that is employed in both North Korea and South Korea today. However, the alphabet was not immediately in use after it was developed. The Korean alphabet system, as a matter of fact, was initially frowned upon by the Korean elite, scholars and officials, who considered the alphabet-based system vulgar and inferior. Over the centuries afterwards, attitudes towards Hangul changed and the writing system became more widely used gradually due to its simplicity and effectiveness. The writing system also has good phoneme-to-character correspondence. At some point, it was not uncommon to see the juxtaposition of Hangul and Chinese characters in one piece of writing. The mixed use of the two writing systems, for some time, was seen in newspapers and other documents. However, now, Korean is written almost exclusively in Hangul or the Korean alphabet and the presence of Chinese characters is minimal/almost invisible. Since many Korean words may turn out to look the same when written using the alphabetic system, Chinese characters are in general only occasionally used to help avoid confusion for certain clarification purposes.

In addition to China's long-standing historical influence on the Korean peninsula, Korea more recently has been influenced by European countries, the Russian Empire, the Japanese and also notably the United States (Brazinsky 2007; Robinson 2007). In particular, over recent decades, American and Western systems, ideology, culture and language have had a profound impact notably on South Korea. As a result, in current-day South Korea, as far as vocabulary is concerned, in addition to core native Korean words and words with Chinese origin, borrowings from English and other Western languages are highly noticeable in recent decades. Also, English in general is becoming increasingly visible and popular and is of great importance in South Korea (Kim 2022; Lawrence 2012) on different levels. Indeed, English is loaded with symbolic prestige and its impact has been labelled as 'English fever', with the appearance of hagwon schools, English villages, 'wild goose' (partial) families living abroad and so on. Please see Schneider (2014) for more detailed discussions on the role and significance of English in South Korea and see Rüdiger (2019) for features and patterns in spoken Korean English. In comparison, for ideological reasons, Korean spoken in North Korea is significantly less influenced by English and is more 'pure' and conservative in nature.

Over the years, a few scholars have explored South Korea's linguistic landscape (Fedorova and Nam 2023; Lee 2019), including empirical studies that aim to shed light on the role of English (Kim 2022; Lawrence 2012; Tan and Tan 2015) in the Korean context. These studies, however, tend to mostly explore the explicit and overt manifestations of English in the Latin script. Yet, the more covert instantiations of English disguised in South Korea's LL remain largely unaccounted for. As such, this section aims to illustrate how English may be disguised and taken for granted in the Korean alphabet, using photos taken from Jeju island's LL as examples.

In Figure 40, 헤어샵 (he eo syab/hair shop), 스모키버거 (seumoki beogeo/smoky burger), 슬로시티 (seullositi/Slow Citi), 땡큐베리 (ttaengkyu beli/ThanQ Berry), and 파리 주얼리 (pali jueolli/PARIS JEWELRY) are all transliterated from the corresponding English names in a wholesale manner. In the last sign in the

Figure 40 English transliterated into Korean alphabet in Jeju island's LL

Figure, partial transliteration can be found, where '스마일' (seumail) that appears to be pure Korean turns out to be the English word 'smile' disguised in Hangul. Clearly, when transliterated into the Korean writing system, 's' as in 'smile' becomes 스 (seu). This points to a case of epenthesis as a vowel is inserted to fit the Korean system. The insertion of extra vowels is a common phenomenon also found in other examples in the inter-scriptal conversion process – a scenario different from the Russian context as we discussed earlier. In many ways, due to the vast differences between the English and Korean writing systems, when rendering English into the Korean alphabet, various changes need to be made. In this sense, it has some resemblance to the scenarios discussed in the Arabic context.

Similarly, in Figure 41, 더골드 (deo goldeu/The Gold), 더 힐링 타임 (deo hilling taim/The Healing Time), 프리박스 (peuli bagseu/Free Box), 스타벅스커피 (seutabeogseu keopi/ STARBUCKS COFFEE) and 홈스마일 (homseumail/homesmile) are respectively rendered phonetically from the

Figure 41 English transliterated into Korean alphabet in Jeju island's LL

English names, despite the existence of common authentic Korean vocabulary. In the last sign in the Figure, it is a monolingual text written in the Korean alphabet. It reads 커피파인더 (keopi paindeo), which is a transliteration from 'Coffee Finder'. Similar to the earlier examples, when the English word 'gold' is rendered into Korea, it becomes 골드[4] (goldeu), with an additional vowel added. More notably, the Korean language does not have the 'f' sound. Therefore, in the transliterating process, sign-makers have to make do with other elements and available resources in the language's linguistic repertoire and linguistic toolkit to arrive at an approximation. The 'f' sound is usually represented using 'p' (ㅍ). For example, 'coffee finder' becomes 커피파인더 ('keopi paindeo') and 'free box' becomes 프리박스 ('peuli bagseu'). As a result of such changes and transformations, English, when (re)contextualised, glocalised and enshrined into Korean, often takes on new characters and almost becomes unrecognisable from the original form.

While lexical borrowing is often due to lexical gap and out of necessity, clearly, in these cases, English tends to be transliterated into the Korean alphabet in a wholesale manner for various stylistic and ideological reasons. This, for instance, includes the ideological belief that English is the language of modernity, progress, globalisation and business (Piller 2003) and the inter-scriptal rendering of English into Korean is modern, awesome, cool, posh and presentable. A few other examples of the same trend can be found in Jeju island's LL (Figure 42). More examples are also illustrated in Table 5. Again, vowels are routinely added to conform to rules in Korean. For example, when the English word 'guesthouse' is phonetically rendered into Korean '게스트하우스'[5] (ges*euteu*haus*eu*), clearly, additional vowels have been inserted to match the Korean syllable structure rules. The same trend is also observable when rendering 'resort' and 'spa' into Korean as 리조트 (lijoteu) and 스파 (seupa) respectively. The systematic insertion of vowels and other transformations stand in contrast to the neat and relatively straightforward inter-scriptal transliteration practice explored in the Russian examples (often with one-to-one correspondence).

In addition to South Korea itself, this tendency for English to be transliterated into the Korean script is also widely seen in other places with significant numbers of Koreans and/or Korea-related businesses (e.g. restaurants). Figure 43 (left) concerns three bilingual signs in Korean and English found in Korean restaurants and Korean-style salon in China's Hong Kong SAR. Clearly, the English name '2 Kims' Kitchen' is, for example, phonetically rendered into the Korean alphabet as 투킴스 키친 (tu kim seu ki chin), hence another example of multiscriptal English in action. The same phenomenon is found in the Dubai International Airport (Figure 43 right).

---

[4] https://forvo.com/search/%EA%B3%A8%EB%93%9C/.
[5] https://forvo.com/search/%EA%B2%8C%EC%8A%A4%ED%8A%B8%ED%95%98%EC%9A%B0%EC%8A%A4/.

Table 5 Further examples of English transliterated into Korean alphabet in Jeju island's LL

Names in English	Transliterated name in Korea alphabet
M. stay Hotel	엠스테이호텔 (em seutei hotel)
JW Marriott Jeju Resort & Spa	JW 메리어트 제주 리조트 앤 스파 (JW melieoteu jeju lijoteu aen seupa)
Guesthouse Brick	게스트하우스 브릭 (geseuteuhauseu beulig)
You&I Guesthouse	유앤아이 게스트하우스 (yua en ai geseuteuhauseu)
Jeju GoldOne Hotel & Suites	제주 골드원호텔앤스위트 (jeju goldeuwon hotel aen seuwiteu)
Hotel Golden Daisy Seogwipo Ocean	호텔골든데이지 서귀포오션 (hotel goldeun deiji seogwipo osyeon)
Terrace Hill	테라스힐 (telaseu hil)
Top island	탑아일랜드 (tab aillaendeu)
Coffee Street 16	커피스트릿 16 (keopi seuteulit 16)
Jeju Hot Pot	제주 핫팟 (jeju hatpat)
Jeju Central City Hotel	제주 센트럴시티 호텔 (jeju senteuleol siti hotel)
Espresso Lounge	에스프레소 라운지 (eseupeuleso launji)
Harbor Hotel	하버호텔 (habeo hotel)
Green Guesthouse	그린게스트하우스 (geurin geseuteuhauseu)
Hotel Sweet Castle	호텔스위트캐슬 (hotel seuwiteu kaeseul)

Figure 42 More examples of English transliterated into Korean alphabet in Jeju island's LL

To sum up, while certain commonly used words borrowed from English (such as 호텔 or hotel) are widely understood, it remains to be seen whether such extensive, liberal and excessive transliteration from English can facilitate effective and meaningful communication amongst Koreans. Indeed, Rüdiger (2018) highlights the largely negative and/or mixed feelings towards using English

Figure 43 English transliterated into Korean in Hong Kong and Dubai's LLs

loanwords by many in South Korea. Arguably, English loanwords are particularly challenging and are difficult to understand for the older generations. Without doubt, these concrete examples documented in the South Korean context (and beyond) illustrate the pervasive nature of such anglicised LL, thus adding to the preponderance of evidence relating to the all-powerful English (Phillipson 2008) being written in multiple scripts around the world against a backdrop of globalisation, increasing connectivity, neoliberalism, and consumerism (Edelman and Gorter 2010). More specifically, English has a special place in South Korea, due to the US presence in the country (e.g. politically, militarily and economically).

7.9 Japan and Japanese-related Businesses Overseas

Multiscriptal English is also figured prominently in Japan and various Japanese-related businesses around the world (e.g. restaurants, entertainment businesses). That is, English is routinely transliterated into Japanese. This is a common phenomenon found in Japan's linguistic landscape and also in signs featuring Japanese around the world. As an East Asian country, Japan has over centuries been heavily influenced by China and Chinese culture, philosophy and language. As a result of the long-standing historical influence, Chinese characters (or kanji) are visible in Japanese and the Japanese writing system. In the country's more recent history, as Japan was modernising itself, it became more westernised and started to borrow significantly from Western countries and more notably the United States and the United Kingdom (e.g. notions and concepts and sociopolitical systems). Current-day Japanese is written in three distinct scripts/systems. These are Hiragana, Katakana and Kanji. While Kanji (Chinese characters) is commonly used to write words with Chinese origins, Katakana is commonly used to write foreign words, especially relatively recent borrowings from English and Western languages. The role and impact of English in Japan and more specifically Japanese English have been explored in Stanlaw (2004), Schneider (2014), Seargeant (2005) and Sakai (2005), amongst others.

Notably, over the recent decades, the tendency of transliterating English and Western words into Japanese (katakana) is an increasingly widespread phenomenon as far as written linguistic landscape is concerned in Japan and also in other Japanese-related businesses or businesses that target Japanese customers abroad (even when the transliteration strategy is not necessarily due to the existence of lexical gaps). Taken from Bangkok, Hong Kong, Kuala Lumpur and Singapore's LLs, Figures 44–50 are but some examples (out of many), where English is disguised in the Japanese writing system (katakana) using the transliteration strategy. This involves single words (e.g. nouns), phrases and expressions (cf. the 'Happy Valentine's Day' example). Some detailed illustrations are presented in Table 6.

Given the major differences between the two languages, when English is glocalised into the target system, changes and transformations need to be made to fit into the Japanese writing system. Notably, this includes the insertion of vowels, amongst other features (which has some resemblance to the situation that some Italian speakers tend to add vowels when speaking English). In Figure 44 taken from Bangkok's linguistic landscape, clearly, the English word 'club' as in 'Phoenix Club' is (re)contextualised into Japanese as クラブ (kurabu[6]). Vowels have been added to fit into the Japanese writing system and/or Japanese speakers' speaking habits (phonotactic rules). Or similarly, オイル マッサージ (oiru massaji) is transliterated from English 'oil massage'. 'Oil' in English is realised as オイル (oiru) in Japanese, again with another vowel sound inserted. Likewise, the English words 'foot massage' become フット マッサージ (futto massaji), featuring the addition of vowel for the word 'foot'. The same trend of inserting vowels is found when 'body scrub' is phonetically rendered into Japanese as ボディー スクラブ (bodi sukurabu). Similarly, in the 'wash & dry' (ウォッシュ & ドライ) example, the English sound 'dr' is not common in

---

[6] https://forvo.com/word/%E3%82%AF%E3%83%A9%E3%83%96/#google_vignette.

Table 6 English Transliterated into Japanese

English words	Japanese (transliterated from English)	Rough pronunciation
Foot steam	フットスチーム	Futto suchīmu
aroma oil	アロマオイル	Aroma oiru
high selection	ハイセレクション	Hai serekushon
cookies & wafers	クッキー&ウエハース	Kukkī & uehāsu
massage	マッサージ	Massāji
Phoenix Club	フェニックス クラブ	Fenikkusu kurabu
Oil massage	オイルマッサージ	oiru massaji
Body scrab	ボディー スクラブ	Bodi sukurabu
hair cut	ヘアカット	Hea katto
eyebrow design	アイブロウデザイン	Aiburou dezain
hair styling	ヘアスタイリング	Hea sutairingu
Happy Valentine's Day	ハッピーバレンタインデー	Happībarentaindē
wash & dry	ウォッシュ & ドライ	U~osshu dorai
barbeque	バーベキュー	Bābekyū
Curry rice set	カレーライスセット	Karē raisu setto
platform	プラットホーム	Purattohōmu
ticket	チケット	Chiketto
check in counter	チェックインカウンター	Chekku in kauntā

Figure 44 English transliterated into Japanese in Bangkok's LL

Figure 45 English transliterated into Japanese in Hong Kong's LL

Japanese. It is therefore rendered as ドライ (dorai) as a close alternative/approximation for 'dry'. Clearly, when English is transliterated and (re)contextualised into Japanese, it adopts new features, thereby getting local Japanese flavours. These examples discussed here remind us of the examples, for instance, in the Korean context, where it is not uncommon to see vowels being inserted when English is glocalised into Korean.

The pervasive presence of transliteration is also widely found in Hong Kong. In Figure 45, the English expression 'Happy Valentine's Day' has been rendered into Japanese in a wholesale manner in a restaurant sign. In the other sign found in a barbershop in Hong Kong, the multilingual sign lists a range of services on offer. Clearly, the Japanese information tends to be mostly transliterated from English. For example, 'hair cut' is realised as ヘアカット (hea katto) and 'hair styling' is rendered as ヘアスタイリング (hea sutairingu), where vowels are again added at the end. Common words like 'hair' obviously had existed in Japanese for a long time before Japan's gravitation towards the West in the country's more recent history. Such extensive use of transliteration from

Figure 46 English transliterated into Japanese in Hong Kong's LL

English may be seen as ideological in nature, reflecting modern Japan's orientation towards the United States and the West in general. More examples of this trend can be found in Figures 45–48, which are also taken from Hong Kong's LL.

In Figure 49 taken from Kuala Lumpur's LL, the same strategy is visible. Apart from bottom-up signs (e.g. restaurant sign and food item), English transliterated into Japanese (Katakana) can be found in top-down signs enacted in major transportation hubs such as Kuala Lumpur's airport and also KL Sentral station. Reflecting the trend identified earlier, vowels are often added when English is rendered into Japanese. For the 'Katsu Curry Rice Set' example, 'curry rice set' has been phonetically rendered into Japanese as

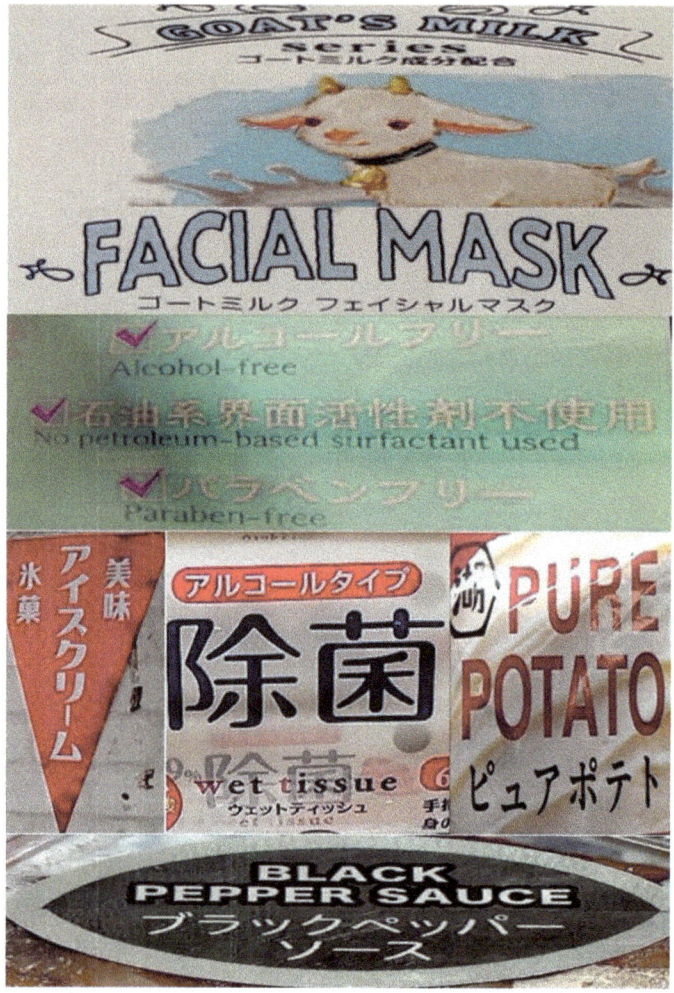

Figure 47 English transliterated into Japanese in Hong Kong's LL

カレー ライス セット (Karē raisu setto), thus giving the English name Japanese flavour. Although the staple food rice has been consumed in Japan for centuries, the English borrowing (rice) is used in Japanese.

Japanese (transliterated from English) is also visible in Singapore's multilingual LL (Figure 50). This, inter alia, includes top-down road signs and signage in the Singapore Changi airport. As a continuation of the linguistic practice in Japan, in Singapore's LL, Katakana is routinely used to transliterate words in English. Notably, the place name 'East Coast Park' is rendered phonetically into Japanese (Katakana) as イースト コースト パーク (Īsuto kōsuto pāku), featuring a few added vowels. This is despite the fact that the place name can be easily rendered into Japanese semantically using Kanji (Chinese characters) as 東海岸公園.

Figure 48 English transliterated into Japanese in Hong Kong's LL

As with other examples, such privileging of sound (as opposed to meaning) points to the power of English and issues of language choice and linguistic ideology witnessed in Japan over recent decades (away from the traditional practice of drawing wisdom from China and Chinese). While this phenomenon is to some extent acceptable in Japanese and many words and expressions from English have become somewhat nativised (and sometimes Japanese speakers might not even be aware that certain words and expressions are from English), these are nonetheless salient examples of multiscriptal English. This illustrates how English gets a second life when (re)contextualised onto and disguised in LLs featuring Japanese, even in places away from the Japanese-speaking heartland. The widespread presence of multiscriptal English written in the

Figure 49 English transliterated into Japanese in Kuala Lumpur's LL

Japanese script is particularly fascinating, considering the situation that many Japanese people have relatively low proficiency in English (as backed up by tourists' general experience of visiting Japan and the EF English Proficiency Index in 2023 which designated Japan as a 'low proficiency' country).

7.10 United Kingdom

Partly for historical reasons and partly because of globalisation, migration and increased mobility, many parts of Europe, North America and Asia are increasingly multilingual and multicultural, becoming dynamic linguistic contact zones and locales of superdiversity (Blommaert 2013; Piller 2018; Vertovec 2007). It is not uncommon to see ethnically diverse neighbourhoods and even ethnic enclaves in our urban spaces. El Raval in Barcelona, Southall, Brick Lane and Edgware Road in London, Sparkhill in Birmingham, Rusholme and Longsight in Manchester, Chinatown in Liverpool, 'Chinatown' and 'Little Italy' in New York City, Box Hill in Melbourne and 'Little Africa' in and around Guangzhou's Xiaobei (Gu 2024a) are examples of this. This, without

Figure 50 English transliterated into Japanese in Singapore's LL

doubt, gives rise to new sociolinguistic realities and cultural dynamics, where complex and hybridised identities are enacted and forged. In the UK, for example, Multicultural London English or MLE (Cheshire, Hall, and Adger 2017; Kircher and Fox 2019) is an example of such new linguistic reality. In a context of globalisation and increased mobility, what appears to be foreign in a far-away 'elsewhere' is in many ways 'next door' in our multilingual and multicultural urban spaces (Cronin 2006: 17).

In this section, 'multiscriptal English' is explored in the UK, a core norm-providing and inner-circle country as far as the English language is concerned. This section shows how English may take on new forms and manifestations in various scripts in the very birthplace and heartland of the English language due to globalisation, sustained migration and increasing linguistic contact. To this end, London, Manchester and Edinburgh, three major British cities, are used as entry points for illustrative purposes.

London

London, a major global city, represents a multilingual and superdiverse urban space. Edgware Road is a major road in London to the north-west of Marble Arch. Known as 'Little Cairo' or 'Little Beirut', Edgware Road is London's 'Arab street'. Featuring middle-eastern restaurants, shisha bars, barbershops, travel agencies, pharmacies, clinics and stores, this street is a thriving enclave made up of Arabs from Egypt, Lebanon, Syria, Algeria, Iraq, Yemen, Sudan and so on who came to the UK for various political, social, humanitarian and economic reasons. This street is also popular amongst Middle East tourists from oil-rich countries who visit London especially in summer to escape the gulf heat. Multiscriptal English is visible to a small degree in the broader area.

A barbershop off the Edgware Road is such an example (Figure 51). Its English name is SALON VICTORIA and its Arabic name is 'صالون فيكتوريا' [saloon fiktooriya]. The lexical items in the Arabic version are both Western in origin. Rather than coming up with separate pure Arabic names for the barbershop, transliteration is employed. As discussed in Dubai, Abu Dhabi and Doha, the 'v' sound cannot be represented using the existing Arabic alphabet. Instead, the 'f' sound is used as an alternative.

Figure 51 Barbershop sign in London featuring inter-scriptal transliteration

Overall, as far as LL is concerned, this ethnic enclave features great authenticity. That is, despite being an enclave carved out of an English-speaking country, overall, authentic, pure and informative Arabic is visible on most bottom-up signs along the road (which focuses on conveying information semantically). This overall more authentic use of Arabic in London is similar to the LLs in other Arabic enclaves for example in Bangkok (Gu and Bhatt 2024) and Kuala Lumpur (Gu and Coluzzi 2024). This is in contrast to Dubai's LL, which features a significant proportion of Arabic signs transliterated from English (cf. Gu and Almanna 2023).

The strategy of transliteration is more commonly found in Brick Lane and the surrounding areas in East London. This area, for historical reasons, has established itself as a centre of British Bangladeshi and other Muslim communities (Rasinger 2007). Over the past few decades, many migrants moved to this area especially from Bangladesh and other Bengali-speaking areas for example in India. A significant number of immigrants in this area are originally from Sylhet in current-day Bangladesh. Initially an ethnic enclave known as a 'Banglatown', now the place has transformed itself and became more gentrified, touristy and commodified after years of development (Rasinger 2007). Apart from curry houses and South Asian confectionery shops, this area boasts cafes, boutique shops, vintage clothing stores and is known for colourful graffiti, murals and various forms of street art made by home-grown and international street artists such as Banksy.

Unsurprisingly, in the area, many signs are written in Bengali. Bengali is an eastern Indo-Aryan language and the Bengali script, derived from the Brahmi alphabet, is closely related to Devanagari alphabet. The script is believed to be a syllabic alphabet that represents the sounds of the Bengali language. While there is a general level of correspondence between the script and the English writing system, precise one-to-one correspondence is not possible in all cases. The existence of Bengali signs gives this area an important cultural and sociolinguistic identity and a sense of authenticity, indexing the fact that this used to be and to some extent still is the heart of the British Bangladeshi community. Interestingly, as opposed to using translation, transliterating is extensively used in signs around Brick Lane and surrounding areas. This is illustrated in Figure 52. In the first sign, the Bengali name is ব্রিক লেন (Brika lēna), which is rendered phonetically from 'BRICK LANE'. Similarly, in the second sign, the English name is 'FASHION ST'. This is transliterated and realised in Bengali as ফ্যাশন স্ট্রিট (phyāśana striṭa). This is despite the existence of common and 'authentic' words such as রাস্তা (rāstā) to mean a road or street in Bengali. In the third sign, again the Bengali name ইস্ট এন্ড কমিউনিটি স্কুল (isṭa ēnḍa kami'uniṭi skula) is rendered from 'East End Community School' in a wholesale manner. In the rest of the

Figure 52 English transliterated into Bengali script in London's Brick Lane and surrounding areas

signs, this transliteration strategy is also visible. While the street signs featuring Bengali seemingly indicate a sense of ethnolinguistic identity and authenticity, these signs fascinatingly tend not to be authentic Bengali but English disguised in the Bengali script. This results in Anglicised LL written in the Bengali script. As discussed in other scripts before, when (re)contextualised in the local script, English adopts new flavours.

Manchester

Multiscriptal English is also extensively found in Manchester, especially into the Urdu script in various Pakistani communities/areas. In Manchester, such areas as Cheetham Hill Road, Longsight, and Rusholme (Wilmslow Road) feature many Pakistani and other South Asian and Middle East businesses (e.g. restaurants, halal meat shops, supermarkets, garment shops, barbershops). In particular, the stretch of Wilmslow Road in Rusholme is known as 'Curry Mile' locally due to the sheer number of Pakistani, Indian, Afghani, Turkish, Kurdish and Middle Eastern restaurants and other businesses. Drawing on data from Manchester's Cheetham Hill Road, Longsight and Rusholme (Wilmslow Road) areas, I show how English morphs into Urdu using examples.

In Figure 53, the Urdu texts are respectively rendered from 'MUSHTAQ HALAL MEAT', 'Pakistani Community Centre', 'PTI CASH & CARRY',

Figure 53 English transliterated into Urdu script in Manchester

'Pakistani Community Center (Longsight)' and 'Manchester Muslim Funeral Committee'. For instance, 'مانچسٹر مسلم فیونرل کمیٹی' [manchstr mslm fiunrl kmiti] is rendered from 'Manchester Muslim Funeral Committee'. Clearly, words like 'meat', 'community', 'centre', 'funeral' and 'committee' are rendered phonetically, despite the often existence of authentic and pure khalis Urdu equivalents (e.g. pure Urdu with Persian and Arabic origins).

Similarly, this phenomenon is also widely seen in food items on menus/products. Figure 54 is extracted from a large menu in a Pakistani-style South Asian restaurant in Manchester's 'Curry Mile'. Clearly, the English names 'RUSSIAN SALAD', 'MILK SHAKE', 'SWEET CORN' have been transliterated into the Urdu script. Interestingly, the English name 'COFFEE' on the menu is rather plain and unmarked. The Urdu version is rendered from the English version yet is more descriptive and detailed, which becomes 'ہاٹ کافی' [haat kaafi] or 'hot coffee'. In the Urdu versions of the food items 'SPECIAL LAHORI PAAN' and 'FRUIT CHAAT', the English words 'special' and 'fruit' have also been transliterated into the Urdu script.

Similarly in Figure 55 (left), a large menu indicating the dishes available can be found in a restaurant in the Curry Mile. Several words in the Urdu

Figure 54 English food names transliterated into Urdu script in Manchester

Figure 55 English transliterated into Urdu menu and food product in Manchester

menu are actually from English. These include 'ٹرڈیشنل لیم' ['trdishnl leem' or 'traditional lamb'], 'ٹرڈیشنل چکن' ['trdishnl chkn' or 'traditional chicken'] and 'اسپیشل' ['ispishl' or 'special']. In Figure 55 (right), it shows the package of a spice and lentil mix for cooking haleem, a dish commonly eaten in parts of South Asia. The package is multilingual, featuring English, French and Urdu. However, the Urdu version, which reads 'kuiik kuk haleem miks' is largely transliterated from English 'Quick Cook Haleem Mix'.

English words also are often written in the Urdu script and appear together with other authentic Urdu elements. This results in language mixing at different levels. Figure 55 (left) discussed above is an example of this. Also, in Figure 56, the first sign (white background) 'حلال گوشت اینڈ پولٹری' [halal gosht aind pooltri] or 'halal meat and poultry' contains the authentic Urdu word 'gosht' which means 'meat'. However, English is also figured prominently in the sign. For example, 'اینڈ' 'and' and 'پولٹری' 'poultry' are simply English disguised in the Urdu script. A similar trend can be found in the second sign in Figure 56. While overall the texts are in Urdu, words from English such as 'VICTORY TAILORS', 'readymade'

Figure 56 Elements of English transliterated into Urdu script in Manchester

and 'waistcoat' have made their way into the text in the seemingly 'exotic' Urdu script.

In the next Figure (Figure 57), it is a 'monolingual' sign in Urdu found in a shop on Cheetham Hill Road in Manchester which details the products and services available. The sign basically says 'Pakistani, Indian, Punjabi films are available for rent. Duplicate service is also provided. CDs, audio cassette, fax, copy, scanning'. Despite the seemingly inscrutable Urdu script used, the content is very 'English' or Anglicised. That is, English words such as 'Indian', 'film', 'duplicate service', 'CDs', 'audio', 'cassette', 'fax', 'copy' and 'scanning' have been transliterated into Urdu. 'Duplicate service', for example, is inter-scriptally rendered as ڈپلیکیٹ سروس (dpliikiit srws). As such, English gets a new life in the new environment.

This is also similarly found in Figure 58, which is a bilingual sign in English and Urdu in a pharmacy/health service provider on and around Cheetham Hill Road. Given the technical and specialised nature of the communication (e.g. health and medical matters), many English words appear in the Urdu script. These include 'blood pressure check' بلڈ پریشر '(bld priishr chiik), 'surgery' سرجری (srjri) and 'cigarette' سگریٹ 'چیک

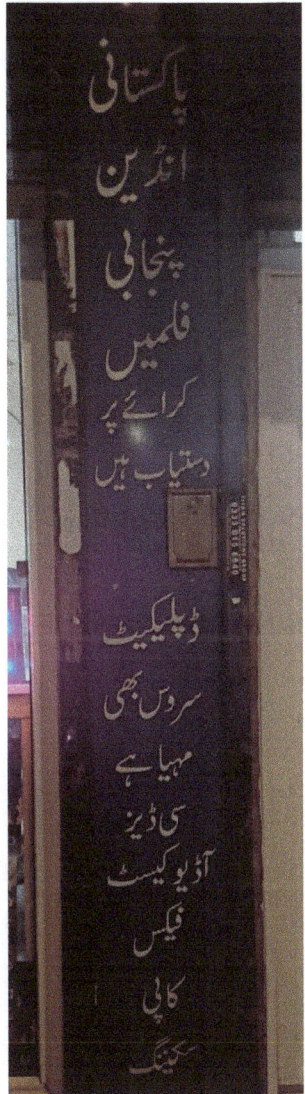

Figure 57 English words transliterated into Urdu business sign

(sgriit). Since current-day India and Pakistan used to be British colony, English has had contact with South Asian languages (e.g. Urdu) for an extended period of time. Arguably, these English words written in the Urdu script are more established and understood in the South Asian context, compared with many (one-off) signs illustrated in Dubai and Abu Dhabi (e.g. CITY VAPE, BLACK & BLUE, JUST FRESH, DAY TO DAY, 'I want to travel the world with you').

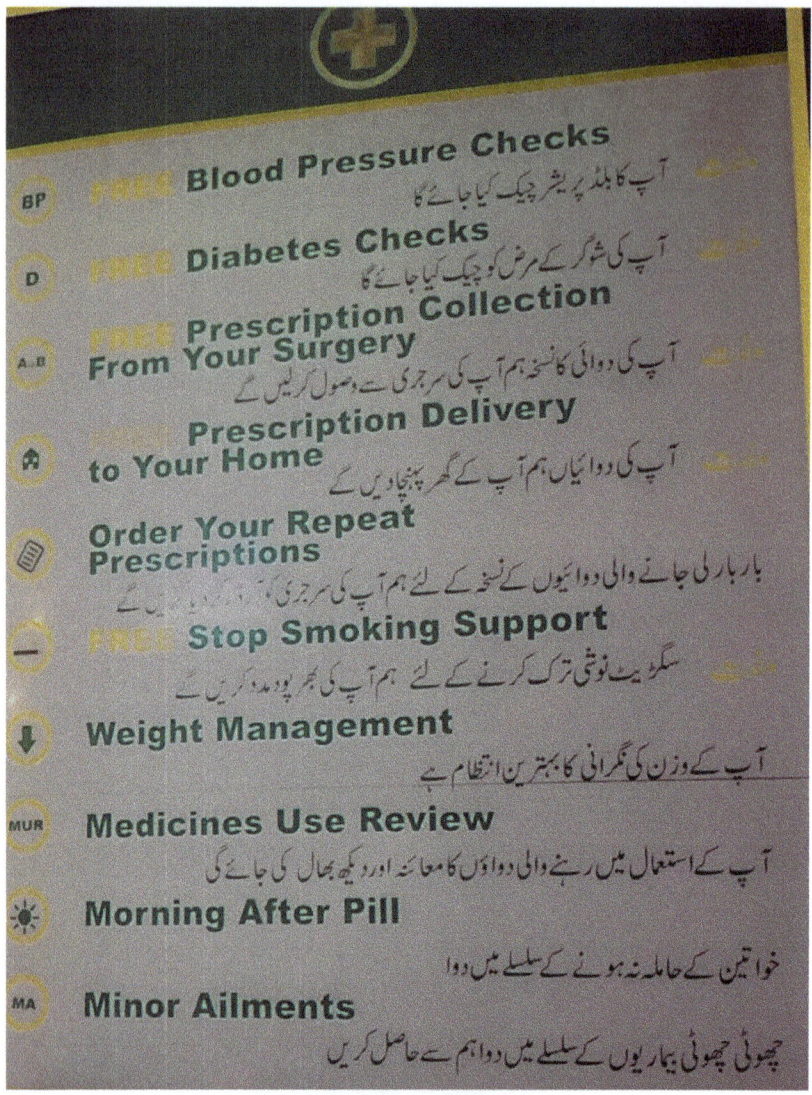

Figure 58 English words transliterated into Urdu in a health-related business

Edinburgh and Beyond

The strategy of transliterating English into other languages/scripts is also visible in Edinburgh. This is illustrated in an ethnic shop located right next to the Nicolson Square Gardens. This shop is called BISMILLAH FOOD STORE (cf. Figure 59 top). The shopfront is multilingual, featuring such languages as English, Urdu, Malay/Indonesian and other South Asian languages. For example, the Malay/Indonesian text 'di sini boleh di dapati daging halal' (here halal meat can be found) is visible (right-hand side at the corner).

Multiscriptal English and Transliteration

Figure 59 English transliterated into Urdu in Edinburgh

Notably, in the Urdu text in red written in the cursive calligraphic style, it says 'bismillah food stoor' (transliterated from English 'BISMILLAH FOOD STORE'). The same strategy can also be found in the Urdu text on the left-hand side of the shopfront. Figure 59 (bottom) is a close-up of the Urdu text. It reads 'halal food shap'. Clearly, this is rendered from English 'halal food shop'. This is despite the existence of common Urdu words to convey the meaning. 'کھانا' (khana) and 'دکان' (dukaan), for example, are the authentic words in Urdu for 'food' and 'shop/store' respectively. This is consistent with other Urdu signs found elsewhere (e.g. Hong Kong and Manchester), where sign-makers extensively transliterate English into the Urdu script.

There are many similar examples of such Urdu signs (transliterated from English) visible in places across the UK (e.g. Birmingham, Leicester, Bradford, Blackburn, Manchester, Oldham, Rochdale, Nottingham, Sheffield). These Urdu signs tend to be written in traditional calligraphic styles such as the Nastaliq style (the Nastaliq style is commonly used to write Urdu and Persian). These signs appear to be highly Islamic/religious, yet the contents are English in disguise. The two signs (Figure 60) are from the same shop in Blackburn's Whalley Range, an area with a significant number of British South Asians. Despite the cursive and exotic-looking calligraphic style, the sign on the left says 'islamik bk siintr' (Islamic Book Centre) and the sign on the right says 'islamik bk siintr aiind freem haus' (Islamic Book Centre and Frame House) respectively. Interestingly, the English word 'book' is repeatedly rendered as 'bk' in the Urdu script with the vowel deleted. This is the same as in the 'TAYAJI ISLAMIC BOOK CENTER' example seen in the example found in

Figure 60 English transliterated into Urdu in an Islamic book shop in Blackburn

Hong Kong. By deleting the vowel, this seemingly gives rise to a kind of ambiguity and fuzziness on the surface, as it is open to interpretation what the original word in English is (e.g. book, beak or back). Indeed, theoretically, the word 'book' could have been more explicitly rendered as بوک (or 'buk') using the Urdu script. This can be achieved in a similar way as in the transliterating strategy found in the rendition of 'food' as in 'BISMILLAH FOOD STORE' – to spell things out. Of course, it is not possible to speculate why the vowel is deleted in transliterating 'book' into Urdu. However, it is possible that rendering 'book' as 'bk' in the Urdu script, while idiosyncratic and random at the beginning some time ago, the practice adopted by the first transliterator(s) gradually became widely accepted. That is, it might have just stuck as a commonly understood and localised way of writing the English word 'book' in Urdu. This observation is seemingly further supported by other sources. For example, Rekhta is a website dedicated to Urdu literature, language and culture (https://www.rekhta.org/). On the website, a section is called 'URDU BOOK REVIEW' (cf. Figure 61). The corresponding Urdu name is transliterated from English as اردو بک ریویو (urdu bk riiuiiu). Again, 'book' is rendered as 'bk'. Similarly, the English word bookmark is represented as بک مارک (or 'bkmark') in the Urdu script. We can tell that such a rendition is widely accepted in the Urdu-speaking world. This rendition is also combined with other words to form words using the Urdu script (e.g. book review and bookmark). This seemingly suggests that initially subjective/idiosyncratic transliteration over time possesses the potential to become accepted and consolidated as part of the language.

Overall, these examples point to the fact that what appears to be Islamic and highly religious actually turns out to be, for example, Anglo-Saxon/Germanic in origin. These real-world examples add to the phenomenon of 'multiscriptal English' explored in this Element.

Figure 61 A screenshot of the Rekhta website

8 Transliterated Globalisation: Some Reflections

Having conceptualised and theorised 'multiscriptal English', I would like to also provide some fresh and much-needed reflections on the idea of globalisation. While de-globalisation is sometimes heard in certain countries these days, in the long run, an interconnected and globalised world will still remain an important fact of life in the twenty-first century. Without doubt, globalisation has fundamentally shaped and conditioned almost every single aspect of our existence. The impact of globalisation is far-reaching, which can be felt in areas ranging from education to business, from technology to culture, and from tourism to entertainment. As such, globalisation is very much multidimensional and multifaceted so much so that even the plural form 'globalisations' is frequently used in view of the inherent complexity and multiplicity of the idea. In other words, to some extent, simultaneously multiple globalisations are in existence in our increasingly complex world, rather than just one particular globalisation in an essentialist or reductionist sense.

For instance, there are economic globalisation, political globalisation and cultural globalisation. In addition, from the perspective of anthropology, Mathews (2008) advances the conceptualisation of low-end globalisation, which is positioned as opposed to high-end globalisation. Unlike high-end globalisation that is characterised by the transnational flow of high-end brands, goods and services (e.g. Tesla, Apple, Starbucks, Amazon, Coca-Cola, Louis Vuitton, Morgan Stanley, Chanel, Balenciaga, Samsung, Google), low-end globalisation refers to the transnational flow of business, trade and people at the more grass-roots level that is less formal, sophisticated and glamorous and involves relatively low amounts of investment and capital (e.g. the trading and selling of cheap t-shirts, shoes, watches and mobile phone cases). The Yiwu wholesale market, Guangzhou's 'Little Africa', Hong Kong's Chungking Mansions, Dubai's Dragon Mart, Bangkok's Soi Arab, Indra Square and Phahurat Market exemplify such low-end globalisation. Similarly, neoliberal globalisation is also commonly used these days to emphasise the kind of globalisation that focuses on a market-driven ideology and competition. Neoliberal globalisation is extensively discussed in many areas, including marketing, business, commerce, education and the health sector (Gupta 2018; Manan and Hajar 2022; Shahmanesh 2007). Also, in the book edited by Ben-Rafael and Ben-Rafael (2018), the term 'multiple globalizations' is explicitly used to signify the multiplicity and multi-layeredness of the idea.

To date, globalisation remains significantly less theorised from a (socio)linguistic and cross-linguistic perspective, if at all. This is despite the fact that language and cross-lingual communication in general is part and parcel of globalisation. In other words, language represents a main thread that is integral to all globalisations. Notably, translation in general is intimately involved in the making of our globalised and interconnected world. This is evidenced saliently in our cities. So far, a number of scholars have argued that our multilingual and multicultural urban spaces in the twenty-first century represent important translation zones and translated spaces (Cronin and Simon 2014; Simon 2012) and, more recently, translational landscape (Song 2023).

While such observations are very much correct overall, I would like to highlight that in many ways our multilingual and increasingly superdiverse world is notably a transliterated space especially against a backdrop of globalisation and neoliberalism (Gu and Manan 2024). This leads us to the concept of 'transliterated globalisation' I would like to advance and develop in the work. As the documented evidence from multiple contexts has tellingly shown, the transference of sound is increasingly prioritised over the conveyance of meaning in a traditional and purist sense. In other words, in many cases, as opposed to resorting to translation in a strict and narrow sense, transliteration is increasingly the go-to practice in meeting the communication needs arising from globalisation. As a result, the resulting versions are not two pure forms but essentially English written in different scripts. Arguably, this increasingly ubiquitous practice, love it or loathe it, may be viewed as a challenge to many old-school and traditional translation theories advocating and foregrounding accuracy, faithfulness and equivalence in rendering meaning semantically between formally defined named languages (where transliteration should only be used for example in rendering certain names without equivalents in another language).

Such transliterated globalisation involves largely the flow of information from the dominant languages (e.g. English) into other less dominant ones, as this Element has convincingly demonstrated. However, it does also happen the other way around to a lesser extent. As alluded to earlier, this inter-scriptal and phonetic rendition is of particular salience on many different levels. That is, firstly, this is often carried out rather systematically not just at a lexical level but also at phrasal and sentential levels (e.g. 'Let's Go', 'Phone to go', 'UP AND RUNNING', 'Origin of Great Taste', 'Cold Halal Chicken Mutton & Beef', 'YES TO LESS', 'Executive Grooming For Men' and 'I Want to Travel the World with You') in many post-colonial, diverse and globalised societies' linguistic landscapes, thus blurring and even uprooting our traditional understandings of what constitute separate languages. Also, what is salient is that in many cases resorting to transliteration is not really due to untranslatability or an inherent lack of corresponding vocabulary but is more of an ideologically driven decision. Thirdly, this is particularly fascinating when we consider how globalisation and other relevant forces have managed to bring distant and even seemingly incompatible scripts, languages and cultures together. The use of script is commonly associated with certain political ideologies, religious beliefs, sociocultural worldviews and sociocultural identities (cf. Coluzzi 2022; Pandharipande 2006). From this perspective, this results in a kind of in-betweenness and gives rise to new and hybridised identities that are sandwiched between the 'foreign, international and global' and the 'traditional, orthodox and local'.

The reasons behind such a transliterated globalisation must be complex and multiple in nature, resulting from the dynamic interplay of a range of sociopolitical, historical, practical, pragmatic, symbolic, psychological and ideological factors. Some tentative reasons have been provided in Gu and Almanna (2023), Manan et al. (2017), Mahmood et al. (2021) and Hussain et al. (2022). These notably include the powerful and influential nature of English in our globalised, commercialised and neoliberal world and the belief that transliterating (e.g. English) into local languages and scripts is considered cool, trendy, and fashionable (Aristova 2016; Bylieva and Lobatyuk 2021; Piller 2003), even though this may be done at the expense of more effective and meaningful communication (e.g. conveying the actual meaning semantically). Since a place's LL represents a socially shaped and socially shaping discourse, the (re)contextualisation and glocalisation of notably English tells a fascinating story, indexing and mirroring the importance of English in our world. The joint force of globalisation and neoliberalism, without doubt, can possess vital shaping roles in language, language use, language policy and language attitude (Edelman and Gorter 2010; Gu and Almanna 2023; Gupta 2018; Manan 2021; Phillipson 2008; Rojo and Del Percio 2020). Indeed, English as a powerful language has been widely established and foregrounded as vitally important, prestigious, cool, attractive and commodifiable that can bring development, opportunities and capitals in various spheres and sectors in a context of globalisation, neoliberalism and consumerism (e.g. Edelman and Gorter 2010; Manan 2021; Sah 2021; Sharma and Phyak 2017). From this perspective, a kind of 'neoliberal governmentality' (Manan 2021; Rojo and Del Percio 2020) is at work here. As a regime of truth, 'neoliberal governmentality' represents a powerful form of governance. As a major structuring force, it is like an invisible hand, which works to govern and regulate various agents and social actors' language use and linguistic behaviour on a day-to-day basis (Manan 2021) in myriad ways. It, therefore, serves to maintain and reinforce the logic of the market without governing (cf. Edelman and Gorter 2010 for more discussions on market as a driving force in effecting change on a locale's linguistic landscape). In many ways, transliteration effectively has become a knee-jerk reaction and coping strategy when less dominant societies and languages are confronted with the Western-dominated globalisation. From this perspective, transliteration represents a major technology that serves to make less dominant languages and countries interpellated (Althusser 2014) as subjects and thus become subject to the broader trend of globalisation and neoliberalism.

In sum, as many former colonies and semi-colonies became independent, they were introduced into a new world order characterised by globalisation and/or a neoliberal ideology. In our increasingly complex world, multiple globalisations may co-exist. Based on documented evidence emerging from various locales in the world, phonetic transliteration, often not translation in a strict and traditional sense, becomes a common go-to strategy that is increasingly visible in many societies' linguistic ecologies (as far as publicly visible linguistic landscape is concerned). As such, the term 'transliterated globalisation' is aptly coined to help describe and capture such an interesting phenomenon theoretically and conceptually. Attentive to the (cross)linguistic aspect of globalisation, this conceptualisation permits a closer and more nuanced look at the central role of language in the making of our urban spaces' LL in a globalised and commercialised world.

9 Discussions and Concluding Remarks

As the former colonial language and now a global lingua franca, English is inextricably intermeshed with and is having far-reaching impact on multiple other languages in various writing systems, which goes beyond just the Roman script. Having assembled documentary evidence from various geographical contexts and language families, this Element shows how English is routinely transliterated, glocalised and (re)contextualised into local scripts (e.g. Arabic, Malay, Tamil, Nepali, Urdu, Thai, Korean, Japanese and Russian) and becomes taken for granted as local languages, against a backdrop of globalisation, increasing mobility and language contact, and neo-liberalism in some of our world's (post)colonial, multicultural and/or dynamic societies. This gives rise to hybridity and linguistic and bilingual creativity (Bolton 2002; Kim 2022; Luk 2013; Moody and Matsumoto 2003) in our linguistic landscapes. While all languages to varying degrees involve elements of other languages (e.g. lexical borrowing), what is at issue and of salience here is the often wholesale transliteration of English into other languages/scripts not just at a lexical but also at phrasal and even sentential levels for various stylistic, branding, commercial and ideological purposes. This clearly goes beyond lexical borrowing (which is mostly to bridge lexical gaps). This phenomenon has different levels of acceptability in different contexts. For example, this phenomenon is widely accepted in Japan with significant signs of nativisation.

As discussed earlier, the making of multiscriptal English is a dynamic (re) contextualisation process, which depends on an understanding of the pronunciation system in English, the affordances, constraints and inherent properties of the target script, and also the transliterator's idiosyncrasy and personal style. As such, the same English word might take on different flavours in different scripts. Indeed, even the same English word may be transliterated into the same script differently by different actors. Also, the inter-scriptal transliteration process might be more straightforward between certain scripts (e.g. between English and Russian) than others (e.g. between English and Arabic).

When (re)contextualised and indigenised into other languages using local scripts, English, as a dominant linguistic code, morphs into and even 'passes off' as 'local' in a surreptitious (and also unsolicited) way. This is particularly salient when involving seemingly inscrutable, 'exotic' and 'mysterious' scripts or writing systems (e.g. the Perso-Arabic script and the Devanagari alphabet) that are often believed to embody and reflect diametrically different sociopolitical, cultural and religious worldviews and values. Since power and ideology are often the most salient and effective when their workings are least visible (cf. Fairclough 1989), the phenomenon under discussion here is of particular interest in helping shed light on the power and dominance of English in our (post)colonial and increasingly globalised and neoliberal world. The infiltration and inroads of English into various other less dominant languages/scripts point towards the power of English, beyond the traditional remit and foci of World Englishes (WE) research. Arguably, such transliteration gives English a new incarnation, a 'second' life and a local and hybridised identity in the new context. Once embedded and crystallised in the local scripts, these English words and phrases may potentially become consolidated and even fossilised as part of the 'local'. While at the beginning such phonetic transference of sounds may not make sense and can only communicate meaning in a minimal way (cf. Gu and Almanna 2023), such practice possesses the potentiality to significantly shape the local languages and contribute to the further Englishisation (cf. Kachru 1994) and Westernisation of the local languages in the years and decades to come. This in turn may effect change in other dimensions and aspects (e.g. language policies and linguistic ideology and attitude) of the local societies that are at the receiving end of the powerful English.

Overall, this contribution sheds new light on English from an interdisciplinary, multilingual, multiscriptal, cross-linguistic and trans-national perspective. In particular, the concepts 'multiscriptal English' and 'transliterated globalisation' have been proposed to better capture the evolving nature of the dynamic relationship between English and other languages and the nature of globalisation in the twenty-first century. This therefore permits us to better understand the role of transliteration (often as opposed to translation in a strict sense) in the making of our LL in our globalised world theoretically and conceptually. Since English is so visibly manifested and intimately implicated in other languages in a myriad of scripts, it is paramount for researchers from diverse backgrounds and traditions to join hands and collaborate in a complementary and win-win manner to more sufficiently understand English's place in the twenty-first century. This highlights the need for researchers in World Englishes (WE) and (socio)linguistics in general to get out of the disciplinary comfort zone to expand the scope and remit of WE research beyond English written in the Latin script in a conventional/traditional sense. This contribution consequently calls for a possible multilingual/multiscriptal turn in WE research and closer interdisciplinary and multidisciplinary collaborations between scholars to better establish the reasons, rationales, mechanisms, effects and ramifications of such emerging language use in our highly globalised and interconnected world.

This emerging trend for English to be transliterated into local scripts begs many questions. For example, this prompts us to critically reflect on whether such phonetic transliteration (from English) is really adequate, effective and meaningful in (intercultural and cross-lingual) communication in a globalised world. It also makes us wonder whether the resulting language should be understood as new varieties of local languages or new kinds of world Englishes disguised in non-Roman scripts. This, by extension, invites us to have a re-think in terms of what English, Arabic, Nepali, Thai, Korean, Russian, Urdu and so on are in the new era. That is, as we have examined earlier, rather than being restricted to just certain lexical items with no local equivalents (e.g. Wi-Fi, iPhone, penicillin, Adidas and H&M), it is not uncommon to see meaningful units to be entirely transliterated from English (e.g. 'Phone to go',

'Just fresh', 'Natural hair & Beauty Salon', 'Cold Halal Chicken Mutton & Beef', 'Origin of Great Taste' and 'Executive Grooming For Men'). In certain cases, it is also possible for whole sentences to be rendered from English phonetically (see the 'I want to travel the world with you' example and the 'IT'S A GREAT COFFEE HOUSE' example discussed earlier). Following this logic, can the famous quote 'Stay Hungry Stay Foolish' from the famous commencement speech delivered by Steve Jobs at Stanford University in 2005 be simply rendered into Korean in an inter-scriptal way? Or similarly can the popular slogan 'I'm lovin' it' from McDonald's be phonetically rendered into Arabic, Urdu and Nepali? If we push the envelope even further, can we have, for example, a whole paragraph written in the local script yet the content is entirely transliterated and imported from English? If so, what language is this? More fundamentally, this widely observed trend begs the question what different languages really mean in an English-dominated globalised world in the twenty-first century. Also, on a related note, since this strategy is so commonly practiced around the world, for countries/languages/cultures that resist the intrusion of English and insist on translating content semantically (e.g. Chinese[7]) in a more traditional and purist sense, will this effectively cause obstacles, risk self-isolation, and prevent the country from more in-depth integration into the existing global sociopolitical and economic structure dominated by Anglo-American nations and the West in general? Also, we should never underestimate the potentiality of multiscriptal English (or English-derived words written in other non-Latin scripts) being able to contribute to and enrich the English language in return. For example, recently, in South Korea, an aging society with many single people and DINK couples, it is common for South Koreans to have pets as companions and family members. As a result, 펫팸 (pet paem) is a relatively new coinage in South Korea. The newly coined Korean word 펫팸 'pet paem' is itself a combination of 펫 'pet' (transliterated from 'pet' in English) and 팸 'paem' (transliterated from 'fam' or 'family' in English). This new coinage from South Korea has the potential to be (re)introduced into English as 'pet fam' and may, thus, have even wider currency globally.

Given various constraints and limitations, it is not practicable to cover all languages/scripts. As such, more detailed and systematic discussions of the phenomenon, for instance, in Hindi (and other South Asian languages) are not provided. Since Nepali, Hindi and a few other Indo-Aryan languages (e.g. Marathi, Bhojpuri, Maithili, Rajasthani) use the Devanagari script, the actual

---

[7] In the Chinese context, there is a tendency to emphasise on translating foreign names and concepts, and so on. semantically as opposed to rendering content phonetically. This is both as a result of the nature of the Chinese writing system (which is unlike writing systems such as the Korean and Arabic alphabets) and also driven by ideological considerations to keep the Chinese language and culture relatively pure.

Figure 62 English appearing in Serbia's linguistic landscape (Cyrillic script)

realisations of the phenomenon in these languages are similar/more or less the same. Indeed, when English elements are, for example, rendered into Nepali, these can also more or less be read by speakers of other languages such as Hindi and Marathi. Actually, based on the author's cursory observations, English, for instance, is also to varying degrees disguised in Burmese, Khmer, Lao, Hebrew, Amharic, Greek, Georgian and various other languages using the Cyrillic script (e.g. Ukrainian, Serbian, Bulgarian, Macedonian, Mongolian and Kazakh). Figure 62 shows a few examples of this phenomenon in Belgrade and Serbia in general. Going forward, it is useful for scholars to, for instance, explore the ways in which English is enacted, disguised and taken for granted in other less dominant and even obscure, vulnerable and endangered languages/writing systems. In addition, given the limited space, this Element has only focused on different places' linguistic landscapes. Going forward, more studies can focus on data from other contexts and venues (e.g. newspapers and magazines) to provide a more comprehensive picture of this phenomenon. Also, while this study has pointed out and established the visible nature of multiscriptal English localised in various contexts, it is beyond the scope of this Element to give concrete statistical information in a systematic way. Based on my rough estimate, however, this transliterated use of language from English can account for anywhere between 10 per cent and 70 per cent in business and shop signs in the places examined here (which is particularly visible in the UAE, Brunei and central Bangkok). In Gu and Almanna (2023), Manan et al. (2017) and Mahmood et al. (2021), some statistical figures have already been provided about Dubai as well as Quetta and Khyber Pakhtunkhwa in Pakistan. For instance, taking a random sampling approach, the LL study in Gu and Almanna (2023) shows that approximately 55 per cent of signs examined feature English transliterated into the Arabic script in Dubai. Going forward, despite the inherent challenge, it would be useful if scholars from various locales could attempt to help quantify this phenomenon in a more systematic and comprehensive way, if at all possible. Given the interdisciplinary nature of this work, it is poised to contribute to such areas as world Englishes (WE), linguistic landscape, urban linguistics, translation studies, globalisation studies, linguistic anthropology, and sociolinguistics and applied linguistics in general.

References

Ahmad, Rizwan and Hillman, Sara (2021). Laboring to communicate: Use of migrant languages in COVID-19 awareness campaign in Qatar. *Multilingua* 40(3): 303–337.

Ahmed, Khawlah (2020). The linguistic and semiotic landscape of Dubai. In Siemund, Peter and Leimgruber, Jakob R. E. (eds.), *Multilingual Global Cities: Singapore, Hong Kong, Dubai*. London: Routledge, 185–202.

Al Agha, Bassem A. (2006). The translation of fast-food advertising texts from English into Arabic. Unpublished MA dissertation. University of South Africa.

Alomoush, Omar I. S. (2019). English in the linguistic landscape of a northern Jordanian city: Visual monolingual and multilingual practices enacted on shopfronts. *English Today* 35(3): 35–41. https://doi.org/10.1017/S0266078418000391.

Alomoush, Omar I. S. and Al-Naimat, Ghazi K. (2020). English in the linguistic landscape of Jordanian shopping malls: Sociolinguistic variation and translanguaging. *The Asian Journal of Applied Linguistics* 7(1): 101–115.

Althusser, Louis (2014). *On the Reproduction of Capitalism: Ideology and Ideological State Apparatuses*. London: Verso.

Amos, Will (2016). Chinatown by numbers: Defining an ethnic space by empirical linguistic landscape. *Linguistic Landscape* 2(2): 127–156.

An, Ran and Zhang, Yanyan (2022). Language choice and identity construction: Linguistic landscape of Jianghan Road in Wuhan. *Journal of Multilingual and Multicultural Development*. https://doi.org/10.1080/01434632.2022.2152456.

Aristova, Nataliya (2016). English translations in the urban linguistic landscape as a marker of an emerging global city: The case of Kazan, Russia. *Procedia – Social and Behavioral Sciences* 231: 216–222.

Baker, Will (2012). English as a lingua franca in Thailand: Characterisations and implications. *Englishes in Practice* 1: 18–27.

Ben-Rafael, Eliezer (2009). A sociological approach to the study of linguistic landscape. In Shohamy, Elana and Gorter, Durk (eds.), *Linguistic Landscape: Expanding the Scenery*. New York: Routledge, 40–54.

Ben-Rafael, Eliezer and Ben-Rafael, Miriam (2018). *Multiple Globalizations: Linguistic Landscapes in World-cities*. Leiden: Brill.

Ben-Rafael, Eliezer, Shohamy, Elana, Hasan Amara, Muhammad, and Trumper-Hecht, Nira (2006). Linguistic landscape as symbolic construction of the public space: The case of Israel. *International Journal of Multilingualism* 3(1): 7–30.

References

Blackwood, Robert and Tufi, Stefania (2015). *The Linguistic Landscape of the Mediterranean: French and Italian Coastal Cities*. New York: Palgrave MacMillan.

Blaikie, Piers, Cameron, John, and Seddon, David (2001). *Nepal in Crisis: Growth and Stagnation at the Periphery*. Delhi: Adroit.

Blommaert, Jan (2013). *Ethnography, Superdiversity and Linguistic Landscape: Chronicles of Complexity*. Clevedon: Multilingual Matters.

Bolton, Kingsley (2000). The sociolinguistics of Hong Kong and the space for Hong Kong English. *World Englishes* 19(3): 265–285. https://doi.org/10.1111/1467-971X.00179. hdl:10356/96202.

Bolton, Kingsley (2002). *Hong Kong English: Autonomy and Creativity*. Hong Kong: Hong Kong University Press.

Bolton, Kingsley (2012). World Englishes and linguistic landscapes. *World Englishes* 31(1): 30–33. http://dx.doi.org/10.1111/j.1467-971X.2011.01748.x.

Bolton, Kingsley and Jenks, Christopher (2022). World Englishes and English for specific purposes (ESP). *World Englishes* 41(4): 495–511.

Bolton, Kingsley, Botha, Werner, and Lee, Siu-Lun (2020). English in Asian linguistic landscapes. In Bolton, Kingsley, Botha, Werner, and Kirkpatrick, Andy (eds.), *The Handbook of Asian Englishes*. Hoboken: Wiley, 833–861.

Bourdieu, Pierre (1977). The economics of linguistic exchanges. *Social Science Information* 16(6): 645–668.

Boyle, Ronald (2011). Patterns of change in English as a lingua franca in the UAE. *International Journal of Applied Linguistics* 21(2): 143–161. https://doi.org/10.1111/j.1473-4192.2010.00262.x.

Brazinsky, Gregg (2007). *Nation Building in South Korea: Koreans, Americans, and the Making of Democracy*. Chapel Hill: University of North Carolina Press.

Lawrence, C. Bruce (2012). The Korean English linguistic landscape. *World Englishes* 31(1): 70–92.

Bruyèl-Olmedo, Antonio and Juan-Garau, Maria (2020). Coexisting varieties of English in the linguistic landscape of tourism: The Bay of Palma. *Journal of Multilingual and Multicultural Development* 41(2): 157–174. https://doi.org/10.1080/01434632.2019.1606226.

Bylieva, Daria and Lobatyuk, Victoria (2021). Meanings and scripts in the linguistic landscape of Saint Petersburg. *Open Linguistics* 7(1): 802–815. https://doi.org/10.1515/opli-2020-0180.

Cheshire, Jenny, Hall, David, and Adger, David (2017). Multicultural London English and social and educational policies. *Languages, Society and Policy*: 1–9.

Coluzzi, Paolo (2016). The linguistic landscape of Brunei. *World Englishes* 35(4): 497–508.

Coluzzi, Paolo (2022). Jawi, an endangered orthography in the Malaysian linguistic landscape. *International Journal of Multilingualism* 19(4): 630–646. https://doi.org/10.1080/14790718.2020.1784178.

Cronin, Michael (2006). *Translation and Identity*. London: Routledge.

Cronin, Michael and Simon, Sherry (2014). Introduction: The city as translation zone. *Translation Studies* 7(2): 119–132. https://doi.org/10.1080/14781700.2014.897641.

Crystal, David (1997). *English as a Global Language*. Cambridge: Cambridge University Press.

Crystal, David (2004). *The Stories of English*. London: Penguin.

Deterding, David (2005). Emergent patterns in the vowels of Singapore English. *English World-Wide* 26(2): 179–197. https://doi.org/10.1075/eww.26.2.04det.

Deterding, David and Sharbawi, Salbrina (2013). *Brunei English: A New Variety in a Multilingual Society*. Dordrecht: Springer.

Deuchler, Martina (1992). *The Confucian Transformation of Korea: A Study of Society and Ideology*. Cambridge, MA: Harvard University Press.

Djuraeva, Madina (2021). Multilingualism, nation branding, and the ownership of English in Kazakhstan and Uzbekistan. *World Englishes* 41(1): 92–103.

Eagleton, Terry (2007). *Ideology: An Introduction*. London: Verso.

Edelman, Loulou and Gorter, Durk (2010). Linguistic landscapes and the market. In Kelly-Holmes, Helen and Mautner, Gerlinde (eds.), *Language and the Market*. London: Palgrave-MacMillan, 96–108.

Fairclough, Norman (1989). *Language and Power*. New York: Longman.

Fedorova, Kapitolina and Nam, Hye Hyun (2023). 'Multilingual islands in the monolingual sea': Foreign languages in the South Korean linguistic landscape. *Open Linguistics* 9(1): 20220238. https://doi.org/10.1515/opli-2022-0238.

Filppula, Markku, Klemola, Juhani, and Sharma, Devyani (2017). *The Oxford Handbook of World Englishes*. Oxford: Oxford University Press.

Foley, Joseph (2005). English in . . . Thailand. *RELC Journal* 36(2): 223–234.

Foster, Mannix and Welsh, Alistair (2021). English usage in the linguistic landscape of Balikpapan's main Thoroughfares. *Indonesia and the Malay World* 49(145): 448–469. https://doi.org/10.1080/13639811.2021.1959162.

Gallagher, Kay and Bataineh, Afaf (2020). An investigation into the linguistic landscape of translingual storybooks for Arabic-English bilingual children. *Journal of Multilingual and Multicultural Development* 41(4): 348–367. https://doi.org/10.1080/01434632.2019.1621326.

García, Ofelia and Li, Wei (2014). *Translanguaging: Language, Bilingualism and Education*. Basingstoke: Palgrave Macmillan.

Gautam, Bhim Lal (2021). Language politics in Nepal: A socio-historical overview. *Journal of World Languages* 7(2): 355–374. https://doi.org/10.1515/jwl-2021-0010.

Gorter, Durk (2006). *Linguistic Landscape: A New Approach to Multilingualism*. Clevedon: Multilingual Matters.

Gorter, Durk and Cenoz, Jasone (2015). Translanguaging and linguistic landscapes. *Linguistic Landscape* 1(1–2): 54–74.

Griffin, Jeff (1997). Global English invades Poland: An analysis of the use of English in Polish magazine advertisements. *English Today* 13(2): 34–41.

Grigg, Peter (1997). Toubon or not Toubon: The influence of the English language in contemporary France. *English Studies* 78(4): 368–384.

Gu, Chonglong (2023a). Enacting Chinese-ness on Arab land: A case study of the linguistic landscape of an (emerging) Chinatown in multilingual and multicultural Dubai. *Sociolinguistica* 37(2): 201–229. https://doi.org/10.1515/soci-2023-0005.

Gu, Chonglong (2023b). 'Mask must wear at all times': Top-down and bottom-up multilingual COVID-scape in Hong Kong as a prime site of epidemiological and public health knowledge (re)construction during the COVID-19 pandemic. *Language and Intercultural Communication* 24(3): 195–221. https://doi.org/10.1080/14708477.2023.2225483.

Gu, Chonglong (2023c). A tale of three global cities: A comparative account of Dubai, Kuala Lumpur and Hong Kong's multilingual repertoires evidenced in their Covidscapes as part of Covid-19 crisis and public health communication. *Language and Health* 1(2): 51–69. https://doi.org/10.1016/j.laheal.2023.06.001.

Gu, Chonglong (2024a). The (un)making and (re)making of Guangzhou's 'Little Africa': Xiaobei's linguistic and semiotic landscape explored. *Language Policy*. https://doi.org/10.1007/s10993-024-09689-4.

Gu, Chonglong (2024b). Linguistic landscaping in Kathmandu's Thamel 'Chinatown': Language as commodity in the construction of a cosmopolitan transnational space. *Contemporary South Asia* 32(3): 360–385. https://doi.org/10.1080/09584935.2024.2378442.

Gu, Chonglong and Almanna, Ali (2023). Transl[iter]ating Dubai's linguistic landscape: A bilingual translation perspective between English and Arabic against a backdrop of globalisation. *Applied Linguistics Review*. https://doi.org/10.1515/applirev-2022-0091.

Gu, Chonglong and Bhatt, Ibrar (2024). 'Little Arabia' on Buddhist land: Exploring the linguistic landscape of Bangkok's 'Soi Arab' enclave. *Open Linguistics* 10(1): 20240018.

Gu, Chonglong and Coluzzi, Paolo (2024). Presence of 'ARABIC' in Kuala Lumpur's multilingual linguistic landscape: Heritage, religion, identity, business and mobility. *International Journal of Multilingualism* 1–31.

Gu, Chonglong and Manan, Syed Abdul (2024). Transliterated multilingualism/ globalisation: English disguised in non-Latin linguistic landscapes as new type of world Englishes? *International Journal of Applied Linguistics* 34(3): 1183–1204.

Gu, Chonglong and Song, Ge (2024). 'Al-Hay As-Sini' explored: The linguistic and semiotic landscape of Dubai Mall 'Chinatown' as a translated space and transnational contact zone. *Journal of Multilingual and Multicultural Development*: 1–25.

Gupta, Amita (2018). How neoliberal globalization is shaping early childhood education policies in India, China, Singapore, Sri Lanka and the Maldives. *Policy Futures in Education* 16(1): 11–28.

Hackert, Stephanie (2012). *The Emergence of the English Native Speaker: A Chapter in Nineteenth-century Linguistic Thought*. Boston: Mouton de Gruyter.

Hilgendorf, Suzanne (2007). English in Germany: Contact, spread and attitudes. *World Englishes* 26(2): 131–148.

Hopkyns, Sarah and van den Hoven, Melanie (2022). Linguistic diversity and inclusion in Abu Dhabi's linguistic landscape during the COVID-19 period. *Multilingua* 41(2): 201–232.

Huebner, Thom (2006). Bangkok's linguistic landscapes: Environmental print, codemixing and language change. *International Journal of Multilingualism* 3(1): 31–51.

Hussain, Riaz, Iqbal, Muhammad, and Saleem, Amjad (2022). The linguistic landscape of Peshawar: Social hierarchies of English and its transliterations. *University of Chitral Journal of Linguistics and Literature* 6(1): 223–239. https://doi.org/10.33195/jll.v6iI.363.

Jain, Ritu (2021). *Multilingual Singapore: Language Policies and Linguistic Realities*. London: Routledge.

Kachru, Braj (1992). *The Other Tongue: English across Cultures*. Champaign: United States University of Illinois Press.

Kachru, Braj (1994). Englishization and contact linguistics. *World Englishes* 13(2): 135–154.

Kachru, Braj, Kachru, Yamuna, and Nelson, Cecil (2006). *The Handbook of World Englishes*. Hoboken: Blackwell.

Kallen, Jeffrey (2023). *Linguistic Landscapes: A Sociolinguistic Approach*. Cambridge: Cambridge University Press.

Kim, Sugene (2022). Blurring the boundaries: English–Korean bilingual creativity manifested in the linguistic landscape of South Korea. *English Today* 38(2): 123–131.

Kircher, Ruth and Fox, Sue (2019). Attitudes towards Multicultural London English: Implications for attitude theory and language planning. *Journal of Multilingual and Multicultural Development* 40(10): 847–864. https://doi.org/10.1080/01434632.2019.1577869.

Kirkpatrick, Andy (2007). *World Englishes: Implications for International Communication and English Language Teaching*. Cambridge: Cambridge University Press.

Kirkpatrick, Andy (2021). *The Routledge Handbook of World Englishes*. Abingdon: Routledge.

Kortmann, Bernd and Schneider, Edgar W. (2004). *A Handbook of Varieties of English: A Multimedia Reference Tool*. Volume 1: Phonology. Volume 2: Morphology and Syntax. Berlin: De Gruyter Mouton. https://doi.org/10.1515/9783110197181.

Koskinen, Kaisa (2014). Tampere as a translation space. *Translation Studies* 7(2): 186–202.

Lai, Mee Ling (2013). The linguistic landscape of Hong Kong after the change of sovereignty. *International Journal of Multilingualism* 10(3): 251–272.

Lam, Phoenix (2023). A multi-sited analysis of the linguistic landscape of Hong Kong through a center-periphery approach. *World Englishes* 43(1): 109–124.

Landry, Rodrigue and Bourhis, Richard (1997). Linguistic landscape and ethnolinguistic vitality: An empirical study. *Journal of Language and Social Psychology* 16(1): 23–49.

Lanza, Elizabeth and Woldemariam, Hirut (2014). Indexing modernity: English and branding in the linguistic landscape of Addis Ababa. *International Journal of Bilingualism* 18(5): 491–506.

Lavender, Jordan (2020). English in Ecuador: A look into the linguistic landscape of Azogues. *Journal of Multilingual and Multicultural Development* 41(5): 383–405.

Lee, Jamie Shinhee (2019). Multilingual advertising in the linguistic landscape of Seoul. *World Englishes* 38(3): 500–518.

Lee, Tong King (2022). Choreographing linguistic landscapes in Singapore. *Applied Linguistics Review* 13(6): 949–981.

Lees, Christopher (2021). 'Please wear mask!' Covid-19 in the translation landscape of Thessaloniki: A cross-disciplinary approach to the English translations of Greek public notices. *The Translator* 28(3): 344–365.

Leimgruber, Jakob R. E. (2013). *Singapore English: Structure, Variation, and Usage*. Cambridge: Cambridge University Press.

Li, Songqing (2015). English in the linguistic landscape of Suzhou: Creative, fluid and transgressive English practices in a Chinese city. *English Today* 31(1): 27–33.

Li, David C. S. (2017). *Multilingual Hong Kong: Languages, Literacies and Identities*. Cham: Springer.

Li, Wei (2018). Translanguaging as a practical theory of language. *Applied Linguistics* 39(1): 9–30.

Li, Wei and García, Ofelia (2022). Not a first language but one repertoire: Translanguaging as a decolonizing project. *RELC Journal* 53(2): 313–324.

Lim, Lisa (2004). *Singapore English: A Grammatical Description*. Amsterdam: Benjamins.

Lim, Shaun T. G. and Perono Cacciafoco, Francesco (2023). Naming public transport and historicising experiences: Critical toponymies and everyday multilingualism in Singapore's mass rapid transit system. *Urban Studies* 60(15): 3045–3060.

Lin, Evangeline (2023). Language and tourism in Cambodia: A multi-case study of the linguistic landscape in Phnom Penh hotels. *Asian Englishes* 26(2): 475–497.

Liu, Guangxiang and Ma, Chaojun (2023). English in a rural linguistic landscape of globalizing China: Language commodification and indigenous resistance. *English Today* 40(1): 62–69.

Lou, Jackie Jia (2016). *The Linguistic Landscape of Chinatown: A Sociolinguistic Ethnography*. Bristol: Multilingual Matters.

Low, Ee Ling and Pakir, Anne (2018). English in Singapore: Striking a new balance for future-readiness. *Asian Englishes* 20(1): 41–53.

Luk, Jasmine (2013). Bilingual language play and local creativity in Hong Kong. *International Journal of Multilingualism* 10(3): 236–250.

Mahmood, Urooj, Shah, Mujahid, Qureshi, Abdul Waheed, and Sultan, Neelam (2021). An exploration of the linguistic landscape of district Nowshera-Khyber Pakhtunkhwa: A case study. *Palarch's Journal of Archaeology of Egypt/Egyptology* 18(17): 781–800.

Manan, Syed Abdul (2021). 'English is like a credit card': The workings of neoliberal governmentality in English learning in Pakistan. *Journal of Multilingual and Multicultural Development* 45(4): 987–1003.

Manan, Syed Abdul and Hajar, Anas (2022). English as an index of neoliberal globalization: The linguistic landscape of Nur-Sultan, Kazakhstan. *Language Sciences* 92(101486).

Manan, Syed Abdul, David, Maya Khemlani, Dumanig, Francisco Perlas, and Channa, Liaquat Ali (2017). The glocalization of English in the Pakistan linguistic landscape. *World Englishes* 36(4): 645–665.

Mathews, Gordon (2008). Chungking Mansions: A center of 'low-end globalization. *Ethnology* 46(2): 169–183.

McKiernan, Thomas (2021). The linguistic landscape of a Malaysian border town: How English language is allowed to thrive outside of the law. *English Today* 37(4): 224–235.

McLellan, James (2010). Mixed codes or varieties of English? In Kirkpatrick, Andy (ed.), *The Routledge Handbook of World Englishes*. London: Routledge, 425–441.

Meierkord, Christiane and Schneider, Edgar W. (2021). *World Englishes at the Grassroots*. Edinburgh: Edinburgh University Press.

Mesthrie, Rajend (2019). Indian English in theory and action. *World Englishes* 38(1–2): 155–161.

Moody, Andrew and Matsumoto, Yuko (2003). 'Don't touch my moustache': Language blending and code ambiguation by two J-pop artists. *Asian Englishes* 6(1): 4–33.

Nikolaou, Alexander (2017). Mapping the linguistic landscape of Athens: The case of shop signs. *International Journal of Multilingualism* 14(2): 160–182.

Pandey, Shyam (2020). English in Nepal. *World Englishes* 39(3): 500–513.

Pandharipande, Rajeshwari V. (2006). South Asia: Religions. In Brown, Keith (ed.), *Encyclopedia of Language and Linguistics*. Amsterdam: Elsevier, 564–579.

Pennycook, Alastair (2010). Linguistic landscapes and the transgressive semiotics of graffiti. In Shohamy, Elana and Gorter, Durk (eds.), *Linguistic Landscape: Expanding the Scenery*. New York: Routledge, 302–312.

Pétery, Dorottya (2011). English in Hungarian advertising. *World Englishes* 30(1): 21–40.

Phanthaphoommee, Narongdej and Gu, Chonglong (2024). English passing off as Thai in twenty-first century Thai linguistic landscape. *Journal of Multilingual and Multicultural Development*, October, 1–23. doi:10.1080/01434632.2024.2415399.

Phillipson, Robert (2008). The linguistic imperialism of neoliberal empire. *Critical Inquiry in Language Studies* 5(1): 1–43.

Piller, Ingrid (2003). Advertising as a site of language contact. *Annual Review of Applied Linguistics* 23(1): 170–183.

Piller, Ingrid (2018). Dubai: Language in the ethnocratic, corporate and mobile city. In Smakman, Dick and Heinrich, Patrick (eds.), *Urban Sociolinguistics: The City as a Linguistic Process and Experience*. Abingdon: Routledge, 77–94.

Pitina, Svetlana (2020). English influence on linguistic landscape of modern Russian cities. *International Journal of English Linguistics* 10(1): 61–68.

Poon, Franky Kai-Cheung (2006). Hong Kong English, China English and World English. *English Today* 22(2): 23–28.

Proshina, Zoya and Eddy, Anna (2016). *Russian English: History, Functions, and Features*. Cambridge: Cambridge University Press.

Rai, Vishnu Singh (2006). English, Hinglish and Nenglish. *Journal of NELTA* 11(1–2): 34–39.

Rasinger, Sebastian (2007). *Bengali-English in East London: A Study in Urban Multilingualism*. Bern: Peter Lang.

Robinson, Michael (2007). *Korea's Twentieth-century Odyssey*. Honolulu: University of Hawaii Press.

Rojo, Luisa Martín and Del Percio, Alfonso (2020). *Language and Neoliberal Governmentality*. London: Routledge.

Rowland, Luke (2016). English in the Japanese linguistic landscape: A motive analysis. *Journal of Multilingual and Multicultural Development* 37(1): 40–55.

Rüdiger, Sofia (2018). Mixed feelings: Attitudes towards English loanwords and their use in South Korea. *Open Linguistics* 4(1): 184–198.

Rüdiger, Sofia (2019). *Morpho-syntactic Patterns in Spoken Korean English*. Amsterdam: John Benjamins.

Sah, Pramod K. (2021). Reproduction of nationalist and neoliberal ideologies in Nepal's language and literacy policies. *Asia Pacific Journal of Education* 41(2): 238–252.

Sakai, Sanzo (2005). Symposium on World Englishes in the Japanese context. *World Englishes* 24(3): 321–382.

Schneider, Edgar (2007). *Postcolonial English: Varieties around the World*. Cambridge: Cambridge University Press.

Schneider, Edgar (2014). New reflections on the evolutionary dynamics of world Englishes. *World Englishes* 33(1): 9–32.

Schneider, Edgar (2016). Hybrid Englishes: An exploratory survey. *World Englishes* 35(3): 339–354.

Schreier, Daniel, Hundt, Marianne, and Schneider Edgar W. (2020). *The Cambridge Handbook of World Englishes*. Cambridge: Cambridge University Press.

Seargeant, Philip (2005). Globalisation and reconfigured English in Japan. *World Englishes* 24(3): 309–319.

Shahmanesh, Mohsen (2007). Neoliberal globalisation and health: A modern tragedy. *Critique* 35(3): 315–338.

Sharifian, Farzad (2010). Glocalization of English in world Englishes: An emerging variety among Persian speakers of English. In Saxena, Mukul and Omoniyi, Tope (eds.), *Contending with Globalization in World Englishes*. Bristol: Multilingual Matters, 137–158.

Sharma, Raj Kumar (2018). Globalization as politics of neo-colonization: Teaching English language in higher education in Nepal. *Journal of NELTA Surkhet* 5: 106–112.

Sharma, Bal Krishna and Phyak, Prem (2017). Neoliberalism, linguistic commodification, and ethnolinguistic identity in multilingual Nepal. *Language in Society* 46(2): 231–256.

Shohamy, Elana (2006). *Language Policy: Hidden Agendas and New Approaches*. London: Routledge.

Siemund, Peter and Leimgruber, Jakob R. E. (2020). *Multilingual Global Cities: Singapore, Hong Kong, Dubai*. London: Routledge.

Siemund, Peter, Al-Issa, Ahmad, and Leimgruber, Jakob R. E. (2021). Multilingualism and the role of English in the United Arab Emirates. *World Englishes* 40(2): 191–204.

Simon, Sherry (2012). *Cities in Translation: Intersections of Language and Memory*. London: Routledge.

Snodin, Navaporn (2014). English naming and code-mixing in Thai mass media. *World Englishes* 33(1): 100–111.

Song, Ge (2020). Hybridity and singularity: A study of Hong Kong's neon signs from the perspective of multimodal translation. *The Translator* 27(2): 203–215.

Song, Ge (2023). Towards a translational landscape: A study of Coloane's urban features through the lens of translational spaces. *Translation Studies* 17(2): 352–373.

Spolsky, Bernard and Cooper, Robert (1991). *The Language of Jerusalem*. Oxford: Oxford University Press.

Stanlaw, James (2004). *Japanese English: Language and Culture Contact*. Hong Kong: Hong Kong University Press.

Suntornsawet, Jirada (2022). A systemic review of Thai-accented English phonology. *PASAA* 63: 348–370.

Sutthinaraphan, Kritnucha (2016). A linguistic landscape study of advertising signage on skytrain. *MANUSYA* 19(3): 53–71.

Takashi Wilkerson, Kyoko (1997). Japanese bilingual brand names. *English Today* 13(4): 12–16.

Tan, Shanna Xin-Wei and Tan, Ying-Ying (2015). Examining the functions and identities associated with English and Korean in South Korea: A linguistic landscape study. *Asian Englishes* 17(1): 59–79.

Tang, Hoa K. (2020). Linguistic landscaping in Singapore: Multilingualism or the dominance of English and its dual identity in the local linguistic ecology? *International Journal of Multilingualism* 17(2): 152–173.

Taylor-Leech, Kerry Jane (2012). Language choice as an index of identity: Linguistic landscape in Dili, Timor-Leste. *International Journal of Multilingualism* 9(1): 15–34.

Theng, Andre Joseph and Lee, Tong King (2022). The semiotics of multilingual desire in Hong Kong and Singapore's elite foodscape. *Signs and Society* 10(2): 143–168.

Troyer, Robert A. (2012). English in the Thai linguistic netscape. *World Englishes* 31(1): 93–112.

Ustinova, Irina P. (2005). English in Russia. *World Englishes* 24(2): 239–252.

Vertovec, Steven (2007). Super-diversity and its implications. *Ethnic and Racial Studies* 29(6): 1024–1054.

Walsh, Katie (2006). British expatriate belongings: Mobile homes and transnational homing. *Home Cultures* 3(2): 123–144.

Wright, Laura (2000). *The Development of Standard English 1300–1800: Theories, Descriptions, Conflicts*. Cambridge: Cambridge University Press.

Xiao, Rong and Lee, Carmen (2022). English in the linguistic landscape of the Palace Museum: A field-based sociolinguistic approach. *Social Semiotics* 32(1): 95–114.

Yan, Xi (2023). A study of the resignification of English through the linguistic landscape of a private English training centre in China. *Journal of Multilingual and Multicultural Development*. https://doi.org/10.1080/01434632.2023.2189260.

Yuan, Mingming (2019). Submission and resistance in the English linguistic landscape of Chaoshan: Identity negotiation through English translation in two Chinese cities. *English Today* 35(2): 20–28.

Zhang, Hui, Tupas, Ruanni, and Norhaida, Aman (2020). English-dominated Chinatown: A quantitative investigation of the linguistic landscape of Chinatown in Singapore. *Journal of Asian Pacific Communication* 30(1–2): 273–289.

World Englishes

Edgar W. Schneider
University of Regensburg

Edgar W. Schneider is Professor Emeritus of English Linguistics at the University of Regensburg, Germany. His many books include *Postcolonial English* (Cambridge, 2007), *English around the World, 2e* (Cambridge, 2020) and *The Cambridge Handbook of World Englishes* (Cambridge, 2020).

Editorial Board

Alexandra D'Arcy, *University of Victoria*
Kate Burridge, *Monash University*
Paul Kerswill, *University of York*
Christian Mair, *University of Freiburg*
Christiane Meierkord, *Ruhr University*
Raj Mesthrie, *University of Cape Town*
Miriam Meyerhoff, *Victoria University of Wellington*
Daniel Schreier, *University of Zurich*
Devyani Sharma, *Queen Mary University of London*
Sali Tagliamonte, *University of Toronto*
Bertus van Rooy, *University of Amsterdam*
Lionel Wee, *National University of Singapore*

About the Series

Over the last centuries, the English language has spread all over the globe due to a multitude of factors including colonization and globalization. In investigating these phenomena, the vibrant linguistic sub-discipline of "World Englishes" has grown substantially, developing appropriate theoretical frameworks and considering applied issues. This Elements series will cover all the topics of the discipline in an accessible fashion and will be supplemented by on-line material.

Cambridge Elements

World Englishes

Elements in the Series

Uniformity and Variability in the Indian English Accent
Caroline R. Wiltshire

Posthumanist World Englishes
Lionel Wee

The Cognitive Foundation of Post-colonial Englishes: Construction Grammar as the Cognitive Theory for the Dynamic Model
Thomas Hoffmann

Inheritance and Innovation in the Evolution of Rural African American English
Guy Bailey, Patricia Cukor-Avila and Juan Salinas

Indian Englishes in the Twenty-First Century: Unity and Diversity in Lexicon and Morphosyntax
Sven Leuckert, Claudia Lange, Tobias Bernaisch and Asya Yurchenko

Language Ideologies and Identities on Facebook and TikTok: A Southern Caribbean Perspective
Guyanne Wilson

Multiscriptal English in Transliterated Linguistic Landscapes
Chonglong Gu

A full series listing is available at: www.cambridge.org/EIWE

For EU product safety concerns, contact us at Calle de José Abascal, 56–1°,
28003 Madrid, Spain or eugpsr@cambridge.org.